The

Effective

Elementary School Teacher

The

Effective

Elementary

School Teacher

62712

~ Mary Beckwith

PRINTED IN THE UNITED STATES OF AMERICA

B & P

THE SCOPE AND PURPOSE OF THIS BOOK

The Effective Elementary School Teacher was written for you, a modern teacher on the firing line, faced with all the old problems of handling your class while you adjust to the changing curricula of today's education. This book deals with the actual classroom problems and is written by an elementary school teacher who knows from experience just what you are up against, and gives fresh new approaches for handling areas crucial to teaching success.

• How do you prepare for that all-important first day of the new school year? Do you know how to avoid the mistakes so often made—mistakes that can affect the success of an entire year's work?

• Do you organize your new class so that every child shares and takes pride in its operation?

• What of the class program? Is it planned so it covers the required work and still gives sufficient flexibility to allow for the unexpected?

• Curricula are changing and we have to adjust to them, but if you are confident of your ability to create interest and to *sustain* the interest of your children it matters little what your curriculum demands. You can make your social studies effective whether it's about anthropology or the settlements in the New World. You can make a bird's nest as exciting as space travel.

• *The Effective Elementary School Teacher* gives new emphasis to the importance of research to the modern child and discusses the many media available to help make children familiar with this vital tool.

• Chapter Six is devoted to audio-visual aids and shows the

teacher how they may be used to enrich the teaching of many subjects, and gives some idea of how they work.

• Do you wish you could instill in your children a greater sense of responsibility? Here are specific techniques that help achieve this.

• What can you do in a heterogeneous set-up to deal competently with the two extremes of your class—those who move faster than the majority and those who can't keep up? Specific problems are given and the solutions to them.

• Is "conformity" out of date? Is "permissiveness" the answer? There are always rebels of varying degrees. We discuss the very real problem of discipline in detail.

• Some of us are required to teach our own art and music programs and feel we have little to offer. This is discussed fully, showing how much you *can* achieve in the teaching of the arts.

• Are you sometimes concerned about your relationships with other adults you meet professionally—parents, fellow-teachers, and supervisors? Here are specific ideas that work!

• Then we take a look ahead and see what new experiments are being planned—or are already in operation. Any one of these may appear on the door-steps of our schools at any time so we want to have a good idea of what they're all about.

Remember that the treatment throughout is pragmatic, concrete, and specific, dealing with actual problems that come up in day-to-day teaching and indicating how to handle every one of them.

Whether you are a beginning teacher, or a veteran in search of something new, or discouraged, or a bit awed by all the "new" procedures, this book will be of inestimable value. It will give you new confidence—make you a more "effective elementary school teacher."

Contents ~

vii

others interest must be created — The magic formula for creating interest — How the magic formula varies to fit the subject and the needs of the class — How to create interest without teaching a lesson — The benefits of choral speaking — How to help children who are weak in written communication — What children like to write about — The danger of killing interest — Fun with limericks, nonsense rhymes, original class poems — Children find modern math interesting — A surprising technique that works!

Can one instil an appreciation of music and art without being gifted in those areas? — Music is part of a child's life — Let's start with rhythm — Several rhythm band instruments your children can make and use — Using ap-

*propriate records to encourage class singing — Planning a
songfest — Reading music from song books — How a class
can compose its own songs — Media available for music
appreciation — How to conquer your fear of painting
problems — Planning each step of a painting lesson — Seiz-
ing unusual opportunities for interesting painting periods
— Finger painting — Simple but fascinating puppets —
Dioramas — Guiding the class in art appreciation*

Chapter One ⁓

You and Your New Class

$\mathcal{O}$pening day of the new school year is vitally important. The way you handle this first day determines to a great extent your success with the class for the rest of the school year. Intense preparation is needed in planning the smallest details of the day's program, even to familiarizing yourself in advance with the past records of these children with whom you are going to spend so much time.

PREPARATION IS NECESSARY FOR A SUCCESSFUL START

Much groundwork *must* be done before you can meet your new class with confidence. If you refuse to face it, or just don't bother, you will regret it for the next ten months.

WHAT MUST BE DONE?

Some of the preparatory work can be done late in the previous term when you receive your new assignment and the records of the class that will come to you. This is a very busy time of the year and chances are you won't feel like bothering. But a preview doesn't take long, and if you're blessed with natural curiosity it's rather interesting.

PREVIEWING YOUR CLASS

Take one of those long, lined sheets of yellow paper and head several columns as illustrated below. In some school districts everything of importance about the child is recorded on one oversized card, which makes your preview simpler. Other school districts

1

have several cards all of which are contained in a large folder—not much more complicated. As you take a card, list the child's name in Column 1, reading achievement in Column 2 or 3, math achievement in Column 4 or 5. If the health record seems normal just put a check in Column 6, but if there is a history of asthma, cardiac trouble, diabetes, poor vision, or hearing loss, by all means write down that fact. Unless there is a record of a real behavior problem just check Column 7.

A partial preview of a class entering fifth grade might look like this:

1	2	3	4	5	6	7
Name	*Reading Achievement*		*Math Achievement*		*Health Record*	*Behavior*
	Above or on grade	*Below grade level*	*Above or on grade*	*Below grade level*		
Davis, Jeanne	6–2		5–1		✓	✓
Estes, Doris		4–8		4–8	Asthma	✓
Foster, William	6–0			4–2	✓	Violent temper
Lynn, Debbie	6–5		6–0		✓	✓
Mack, Joseph	4–9		5–2		Myopia	✓

* Note: 6–2 means sixth grade second month. Therefore, a child entering fifth grade with 6–2 reading achievement would be one year and two months above grade level in reading. A child entering fifth grade with an achivement rating of 4–2 in math would be eight months below grade level in math.

A GLANCE WILL POINT OUT POSSIBLE PROBLEMS

In this way you have a bird's-eye view of your new group. It will mean more to you when you get to know the children, but at a glance you can tell where possible problems may arise and be ready for them.

When you start to prepare the record book that will be your companion for the "duration," this worksheet will be an invaluable aid. Use it in the fall when you return a day or two ahead of the children.

FURTHER PREPARATION TO INSURE THE SUCCESS OF THE FIRST DAY

Here are three more suggestions that will help get you and the class off to a smooth start:

The appearance of the room: There are few drearier scenes than a classroom at the end of a summer vacation. You turn the key, open the door, and there are the chairs piled on tables. Not one of your framed prints hangs in its familiar place. Bare walls and streaky blackboards stare at you.

Better stifle that urge to close the door silently and head for the teachers' room for coffee. Open the windows instead. Ignore piled chairs if you can and begin digging for the colorful pictures put away so carefully last June. When the thumbtacks or the stapler have been located you can attack the bulletin board. Now the library table needs a dusting and some eye-catching books. After the boards are washed the place begins to look more livable—yes, livable. Aren't 30 or more people going to spend many months there?

Writing a detailed plan for the first day: When it's time to think of a rest, dust off your desk and chair, sit down, unlock the various drawers, and try to find the necessary tools to *begin* work. Here's the bird's-eye view of the new class—the one you prepared reluctantly before school closed. It will be a great help to you as you plan the coming campaign.

Whether the ideas in the first day's plan are listed 1,2,3,4, and so on, or have the appearance of a short essay, is really immaterial. Most important is your *aim for the day and how you will go about achieving it.*

When allotting time for each activity be generous, for you are not familiar with the peculiarities of these children and things may take longer than expected. (If you find out later that you don't need all the time allotted, plan to use any remaining few minutes for a little informal conversation with the class. Or you might play a game ("What's My Name?" is a favorite) or go right on to the next item in the day's plan.) *Keep your aim in mind* and the jig-saw pieces of the day will fall into place.

Alternate plans prove useful: Here's a handy hint! Always have some alternate plan up your sleeve, whether it's the first day or the hundred and first. Interruptions occur in the best run schools and classrooms—an unexpected visitor, a fire drill, a call to the office. Be prepared with a variety of little subplans:

(a) Have a new poem ready to teach. Tell the children about the poet, too. *But have it well-prepared.*

(b) Be ready with an interesting blackboard game to bridge an unexpected gap. "Hangman" doesn't sound relaxing, but it is—and very handy at times. And then there's always the chance that it might give the children's spelling a boost.

If the interruption should be a call to the office or a sick child— either of which would require your leaving the classroom temporarily—have a crossword puzzle mimeographed and ready to be used.

It's wise to have several "subplans" pasted inside the cover of your plan book, and it's a practical way to avoid that sudden panic when things don't go the way you expect.

THIS IS IT!

Now the big day has arrived. A teacher new at the job may be forgiven for having a few qualms. Would it make it any easier if you knew that even the veterans feel much the same way? Soon there will be no time to think about such things. You'll be carrying out your program, and if it's been carefully prepared you will have things well in hand. You and the class will enjoy it.

HOW TO PASS THE FIRST TEST

In some schools children form lines in the yard or gym. In other schools they go directly to their room. But on the opening day— almost everywhere—lines form in the yard or gym and then proceed to the rooms. *Meet your class,* whether it is in the yard or at the door of your room. If you are known to the children as the teacher of the "next" class there is a definite advantage. If you're new to the school the children are honor bound to try you out. If they're giggly say nothing. Walk slowly up and down the line as if you were inspecting it. Don't be afraid to wear a small smile. Nothing quiets down the fresh ones like a teacher who says nothing— just looks.

TEMPORARY SEATING IS ENOUGH NOW

When the children are attentive, greet them. Send in four at a time, telling them, "Take the seats at the first table (or the first four seats in Row One), just for the present." Stand where you can supervise the group in the hall and the group in the room.

After the last child has taken his temporary seat wait for complete quiet. There may be two or three who have brought coats or sweaters. Let them hang their wraps on any hook for the present. If one pupil keeps you or the class waiting, simply tell him to sit at the library table until he considers himself ready to rejoin the group. Don't raise your voice. You may raise it later, but not during the first hour—or on the first day, if possible.

YOUR FIRST "SPEECH" SETS THE TONE

Talk to your new class for a few minutes. Speak softly so they will have to be attentive to hear you. Give them a very small preview of some of the more exciting things this new grade has to offer. Then introduce yourself.

"Before I tell you *all* about fifth grade perhaps we had better introduce ourselves to each other. My name is written on the board. Some of you may know me because I may have had your older brother or sister in my class.

"I'm going to take this roll book" (show it to them) "and call your name. Please stand so that I may have a real good look at you. If I mispronounce your name please tell me."

Naturally, you will suit the "speech" and self-introduction to the age of your class. I have found this time-tested procedure to be a foolproof technique for starting that all-important first day.

THE FIRST ROLL CALL CAN BE PLEASANT FOR TEACHER AND PUPILS

Take your time with the first roll call. Say a few words to each child. If one of them has the reputation of a demon, never let on by word or look that you know anything about him. Let him wonder how much you *do* know. Perhaps he means to turn over a new leaf this year—it *does* happen sometimes.

TEACHER AND PUPILS LIST SOME NECESSARY ITEMS

See that each child has a pencil and paper. Most parents want their child to at least *start off* right and many of them will have new, long pencils and fresh, clean notebooks. Compliment them, but don't criticize the others—it's not always their fault.

Ask the children to help you make a list of articles they will need in school each day. Write the list on the board and have them copy it on paper or in the new notebook—such items as pencils, notebook, a very *inexpensive* pen, and so on. They may suggest a handkerchief or tissues. Fine! They'll need them. (The first homework will be to have this list signed by someone at home.)

INTRODUCE THE CHILDREN TO THEIR NEW ROOM

Now let's relax and look around the room—this room that you have prepared for the new class. Discuss the bulletin boards and the various colorful pictures you have selected. Let them know that some very lucky people may have the job of keeping these boards up-to-date. There are plenty of good jobs to go around. We'll plan to share the work and the pleasure in our class.

Point out the library corner and give the class an idea of what treasures may be found there. It's good to have a few books with attractive dust covers very much in evidence.

Did you have time to hang any colorful framed prints on the wall? Tell them about the most interesting of the artists. Children love a story!

It's amazing how fast the first hour flies when it has been well planned. If you are still uninterrupted by recess or assembly, have your class take a good stretch. Then see that each child has a fresh paper. Show the class how you expect them to head a paper, and keep this sample heading on the board for at least a week.

.QUESTIONS FOR GETTING ACQUAINTED

Write some questions on the board, such as:

Where do you live?
How long have you lived there?
How many brothers and sisters do you have?
Did you ever go to another school?
What is your favorite subject?
What is your favorite game?

What was the best thing that happened to you this summer?

(Some of the information is on the record card, but this technique helps in getting acquainted.)

Give the children a chance to talk over the questions and be sure they understand them. Walk around the room while they're writing the answers. Notice the ways in which different children tackle the assignment for this can give an alert teacher some valuable hints, and some of the answers are eye-openers. Collect the papers, read them carefully, and keep the set in your file.

PRACTICE LINING UP

During the morning practice lining up. Give each child a temporary number to facilitate the operation. Never mind size places today—that can be done tomorrow or next day. Right now the important objective is a quiet, intelligent (how they react to that word!) procedure for getting on line.

CLASS TOUR OF THE BUILDING

"As long as we're on line, children, and the line looks so good, let's take a tour of the building. I'm sure most of you know where the important places are, but we do have four new class members and as we tour I'll point out these places to them. I'll show all of you which entrance and exit you'll be using and where we'll stand on a fire drill, so be quiet and attentive."

Point out to the children the location of the lunchroom, auditorium, office, nurse's office, etc.

This is an ideal time to emphasize the importance—indeed, the necessity—of quiet in the halls. Tell them that later on in the week you will show them how to make a plan or map of the inside of their school building.

CHECK LUNCHROOM USERS WELL BEFORE NOON

Before lunchtime you will have to check to find out: (1) how many eat at home, (2) how many have lunch in school, (3) of these how many will bring lunch from home, and (4) who will be ordering hot lunch in school. Be sure to take care of this well before the bell sounds.

If there should be a few free minutes before noon dismissal take that colorful storybook from your desk. Show it to the children, discuss it briefly, explain that you plan to read to them as often as possible. The Dr. Doolittle books, for example, are great fun for both bright and slower pupils.

TEACHERS SELDOM RELAX AT NOONTIME

It would be fine to be able to relax at noon and forget your troubles, but this is one blessing teachers do not have. If you are fortunate enough *not* to be on lunch or playground duty you'll probably take a 15- or 20-minute break and return to your desk. Whatever is done now means that much less to be done tonight.

FOLLOW MORNING PROCEDURES FOR SEATING IN AFTERNOON

Many supervisors insist that each teacher meet the class in the playground morning and afternoon for the first week. This is certainly an extra chore, but it does have some obvious advantages.

Whether you meet your class in the playground or at your own door, insist quietly on good self-control before they enter the classroom. Your practiced eye can see, without seeming to, just who is slyly poking whom for a bit of diversion. Separate him—or her—from the others with little or no comment.

Follow the same seating procedure used in the morning. Later this afternoon we'll arrange a semipermanent seating plan. It is a good idea to call the roll again as it gives you another opportunity to associate names and faces that prove hard to remember.

DISTRIBUTING BOOKS

The children will begin to wonder when you're planning to give them some books. Good readers or poor, they love to get books.

Choose two husky boys and have them help you distribute *one* set of books—the most attractive set you have. If you're fortunate enough to own some of the new social studies books with colorful illustrations, by all means let the children have them first. As soon as the book touches the desk their curiosity will have them turning pages. Walk around the room and make a comment to this one, or ask a friendly question of that one, about a certain picture or story. Use any such opportunity to get to know these little individuals.

"TEACH SOMETHING NEW THE FIRST DAY"

The wisest, most understanding supervisor I have ever worked for impressed upon her teachers the importance of teaching something new the first day.

"Teach them something new," she would advise, "even if it's something quite simple. It makes the children feel school is important, and they like to tell their parents about it."

If it's social studies books you have distributed why not discuss with them the interesting possibilities of the "time line"? Older children are able to enjoy making one running from 1492–1776. Younger ones get a real charge out of one that covers their own short life span (eight to ten years).

A class might study together a map of the Americas and trace earliest explorations with your help.

Second graders might learn some new words having to do with objects in their room.

Tell any grade the story of the person after whom their school is named.

ASSIGN SOME HOMEWORK

Assign a little homework—not enough to discourage the fainthearted before they really get started, but enough to let them know you mean business. For example:

1. Take home the list we made this morning and have it signed.
2. Bring in as many of these items as you can.
3. Cover your new book.
4. Read the "Contents" pages and be able to explain their use.

Write the assignment on the board and see that the children copy it.

AN EFFECTIVE SEMIPERMANENT SEATING PLAN

Now to get to a workable yet flexible seating plan. Permit friends to sit together if they request it, if such important factors as hearing loss or poor eyesight do not have to be considered. Don't be too surprised at this suggestion, for friends frequently work well together and make a good team. If they abuse the privilege you will know soon enough and can make the necessary adjustment. In a modern classroom there is so much shifting about for various groupings that the friends may not be together as much as they expect.

The most practical seating plan is to group your children according to their reading ability. Much of their work will require reading and it's simpler and more efficient that way. The preparation you have done for the new class will include a knowledge of just such items as reading ability and any health defect, like hearing loss or poor eyesight, which would necessitate a child's being near the front of the room.

If, in spite of your good planning, it seems the rearrangement is becoming noisy or is taking too long—just stop it. Do it the first thing tomorrow. Don't jeopardize your control of the class simply to adhere to a given plan.

TWO SIMPLE IDEAS TO PROVIDE A BIT OF RELAXATION

1. The children will enjoy playing this game during the first day or two: tell them that you want to see how many of their names you can remember. It's great fun for the class and not as hard for teacher as you might imagine. This little fellow must be Billy T. because he's the image of Jim T., who was in your class two years ago. And this little redhead certainly fits her name, Rosemary, and so on. When teacher is stymied over a name it's the cause of much glee, but it's surprising how quickly you learn to associate names and faces.

2. If you and the class are tired—now, or almost anytime—stop what you're doing, take a good stretch or two, and sing a song. It's wonderful how a song can bring back good spirits and renew the energies. Children love the unexpected, and if you break the monotony of a lesson in this way it pays rich dividends:

For little ones:	*For older children:*
"Twinkle, Twinkle"	"Frere Jacques"
"Go Tell Aunt Rhody"	"Home On The Range"
"Jimmy Crack Corn"	"John Brown's Body"

The song should be familiar to be thoroughly enjoyable and relaxing. As you teach more songs you can add them to your list of favorites.

THAT FIRST SCHOOL DAY DRAWS TO A CLOSE

Perhaps you find that there are 15 or 20 minutes left before the first busload takes off—not enough time to start a new lesson. Ask if someone would like to tell about an exciting event that occurred during the summer. No doubt several children went to camp, or took a trip, or earned money while school was closed. They'll enjoy telling about it.

Use this opportunity to mentally screen the extroverts and the introverts. (Some of the extroverts may already have shown their colors.) You'll be jotting down notes frequently in your own peculiar shorthand—notes that can be an invaluable aid in your future dealings with the children—and the first day is a good time to begin.

Make the "Good afternoons" pleasant and courteous today and every day, no matter how weary you may be. Check to see that each child has his book to cover, and his homework assignment, too. Let them know *today* that each one has a job to do, and that *you expect it to be done well.*

TIME FOR REFLECTION

That vitally important first day has come and gone. Sit at the desk for a few quiet moments, alone in the room at last. Check the plans you made for this day to see if you have been able to accomplish the most important of them.

What do you consider to be the most important accomplishment of the day? Without question it is the rapport established between yourself and the new class. A firm handling of each situation, a fairness that the children will learn to appreciate and respect, has placed you in control, and both you and they will have a good, solid sense of security because of it.

TEACHERS VARY GREATLY IN THEIR ATTITUDE TOWARD A CLASS

Mr. Porter, teacher of a sixth grade, believes in a tough, strict start. "I let them know the first minute who's boss!" he brags. "They don't get away with one thing in *my* room!"

If the truth were known, Mr. Porter loves his "kids" and is a real softy at heart.

Mrs. Janis, your co-worker in fifth grade, is a good, hard-working teacher, but she lacks confidence in her ability to control a lively class. She begins the new school year by ingratiating herself with the children.

"They like me," she says beaming, "and I think they're going to be the nicest class I've had in years."

The poor, dear lady says the same thing every fall and has the same difficulty in maintaining discipline after the first week.

And what about yourself? Are you somewhat concerned that your new class went home without a spelling or math assignment? Don't fret! There's plenty of time for math and spelling. This class understands what is expected of them. Naturally you'll have to re-emphasize certain rules from time to time, but you won't have to rely on nagging or a loud voice. The tone of the relationship has been established. Careful planning and a firm but pleasant attitude toward your class have set the stage for a successful year.

——— GETTING THE RIGHT START ———

Opening day is the most important day of the school year. It is worthwhile making detailed plans for the exact way you will proceed.

When you receive the records of your new class, usually at the end of the preceding school year, make a preview sheet of the children coming to you. This will give you a bird's-eye view of any potential problems in achievement, conduct, or health.

Prepare your room—
    (a) Have attractive bulletin boards.
    (b) Put interesting books on display.
    (c) Hang a picture or two.

Write a detailed plan of the activities you expect to introduce—and accomplish—the first day. The *first few minutes* are vitally important. Have some little "subplans" ready for an emergency.

Meet your class. Be firm but pleasant. Speak softly and as little as possible.

Teach *something* new the first day.

Assign some simple *but definite* homework.

Today, and any day, take time to break the tension and relax with a stretch or a song.

The most important achievement of the first day should be the rapport established between teacher and class.

Chapter Two ⁓

Organize Your Class
and Room

One of the teacher's first big jobs is to organize the class and classroom. This organization sets up the routines within which all the daily activities take place. It covers everything from getting on line to who takes care of the bulletin boards. The routines themselves will vary with the age of the children, the location of the room, and the teacher.

SPECIAL NEED FOR ROUTINES IN THE FIRST GRADE

When a child enters first grade he has to learn many routines before he learns much else. Think of how completely inexperienced a six-year-old is! Does he know the acceptable way to enter or leave his classroom? Put away his coat or rubbers? Does he know how to proceed to the lunchroom or the lavatory? How does he find the right bus? The answers to these questions are important, and head the long list of routines a small child must learn for his own safety and comfort and that of his classmates.

GETTING ON THE RIGHT BUS

Mrs. Harris describes the difficulties met in training her first grade to find *and remain on* the right bus line:

"Fully an hour before the children were to go home that first afternoon I talked with them about buses. Twenty-five of my class of 30 live more than a mile away and there are five buses lined up at the curb—all looking alike and each one having a different destination.

"As we talked about traveling to and from school I displayed colored circles. The children's curiosity was aroused, so I explained that each group going home on a certain bus would wear a certain color. To make it more effective I had printed each child's name and address on his circle—just in case!

"Then we practiced getting on bus lines. That went fairly well— as long as we remained in our room and practiced. I took the children into the hall to show them where each color group would stand and wait for the bus. As soon as I turned away from Kathy's group she calmly joined another line because 'her friend was there.' The fact that she would have landed 12 blocks from her home never crossed her little mind!

"I realized then," continues Mrs. Harris, "that I had to find a simple, graphic way to get them on the right bus."

HOW TO FIND THE RIGHT BUS

1. That night Mrs. Harris prepared a large chart showing the school building in the center with the buses lined up at the curb.

2. Each bus on the chart was a different color, and a line extended in the direction taken by the bus as it carried the children to their homes. The destination was shown by a circle of the same color.

3. The teacher explained the meaning of the chart to her class and told them that they would play a game.

She thumbtacked five colored circles in five different places in the classroom and distributed the correct color to each child. Then she called all the "yellows" to come and stand under the yellow circle, the "blues" under the blue, and so on. This was repeated several times.

4. The same procedure was followed in the hall where they would wait for the buses.

5. There was one possible complication—*all five school buses were yellow!* Mrs. Harris persuaded the drivers to display a large, colored circle (provided by herself) on the side of the bus. ("Just for the first week," she promised the drivers.)

6. To insure the success of the plan Mrs. Harris borrowed five older girls for monitors. Each girl would wear a colored scarf

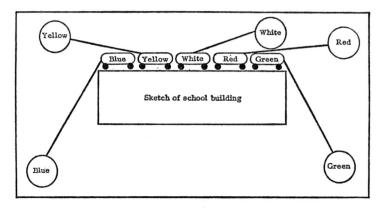

(blue, yellow, etc.) when she called her little group to escort them to the bus.

7. By the end of the first week even the children who had known *no* colors were able to recognize one at least, and were proudly walking over to the bus with the same color on it.

ROUTINES MUST BE REVIEWED CONSTANTLY

First-year teachers can never take for granted that six-year-olds have learned all the necessary routines nor that they will remember them.

"You tell them once," says an experienced teacher of early grades, "and you tell them again and again. Each day you repeat the same instructions—make a game of it when you can. There's no use losing your temper—most of them just don't remember!"

Sometimes we find a class of older children who have forgotten (or never learned) some of the important routines. If such a class comes to you, no matter what grade it may be, stop everything else and teach such routines to them! It will save your time and temper, and it may even save a child's life in an emergency.

HELPING WITH THE ORGANIZATION

Children in the first and second grades are not much help to you in planning your organization—and you should not expect them to be. Sometimes they enjoy the experience of deciding where to set up the work and play centers in the room—at least, the teacher lets them think they are the ones who decide. Sometimes you'll find a good little monitor for a certain job. Once in a while you'll come across a class that seems more able to do things.

AN UNUSUALLY CAPABLE FIRST GRADE

Miss Cort is a first grade teacher of long experience. Her present group of 30 children is, in her opinion, the smartest group she has taught. Their reading achievement ranges from 1-9 to 3-4 *—well above grade level (which was 1-5 at testing time)—and they are quite mature for their tender years.

The teacher finds that 12 of these children are able to perform small monitorial jobs with little supervision. John and Ellen take complete charge of the distribution of papers and books. Peter and Margaret take care of weaving materials and crayons. Larry understands his job as office monitor—at least he can find his way and carry a simple oral message. Gradually, each of these efficient little helpers will train another child to carry on with his duties, and Miss Cort will let John and Ellen, Peter, Margaret, and Larry try new jobs.

SLOWER CHILDREN CAN BE EXCELLENT MONITORS

Mrs. Roberts, who has taught first and second grade boys and girls for 15 years, believes that slower children often make better monitors. She says that it takes longer to train them but they enjoy the sense of accomplishment that it gives them and are more inclined to do classroom jobs carefully. Dusting teacher's desk and the library table are considered privileges. Watering the plants and picking off dead geranium leaves requires the utmost skill, and the child who performs this task feels he's someone special.

"Just one warning," Mrs. Roberts will say. "They'd like to do it all day long. You have to keep an eye on things and make sure they don't overdo the jobs."

OLDER CHILDREN ENJOY ORGANIZING

You will find that children in the fourth, fifth, and sixth grades are eager to take part in the organization of their class. They love committees and work together quite well, *but need direction from the teacher*. It's a good idea to organize them into working committees responsible for the performance of definite duties as early in the term as possible—even during the first week. Have them

---

* See Chapter One.

elect chairmen directly responsible to you for the smooth functioning of their committees.

Let's look in on Miss Cook as she tackles the classroom job assignment. She has a picture in her mind of what she wants, but will it work out that way? She's capable, has plenty of confidence, but can she handle a sticky problem wisely?

FOURTH YEAR CHILDREN CHOOSE JOBS

Miss Cook has been teaching only three years. She's young and peppy and even though she lacks wide experience she loves teaching and seems to be a "natural."

It is the first week of the school year and Miss Cook and her fourth graders have established a few necessary routines rather easily. Now they are discussing the variety of monitorial jobs listed on the board. This class is a medium group—no extremely slow ones and no shining stars—but, as their young teacher boasts, "They have lots of common sense—give me the average kid anytime!"

"Well, children, there it is," says Miss Cook pointing to the list of jobs on the blackboard. "These are the jobs to be done in our room. Some are glamorous and others are just plain work. We've talked about them and you have a pretty good idea of what each requires. I wish you could have the job you want most, but if you don't get it now you'll probably have a chance at it later on. You remember we decided to change jobs every month to give each of you a chance. Now, let's go down the list to find out how many are applying for each position. I'll read the list and you raise your hand when we come to your choice."

(The teacher fills in the number of applicants for each job as follows:)

Job	Applicants	Job	Applicants (new vocabulary word)
Bulletin boards	12	Dusting	0
Attendance	4	Paper baskets	1
Weather and temperature	4	Library	6
Chalk and erasers	6	Art supplies	2
Office	5	Books and book closets	4
Plants	5	Paper and paper closets	3
Host and hostess	4	Hall bulletin boards	2

Miss Cook frowns as they go down the list. It adds up to 58 and she only has 30 on register!

From her earliest weeks of teaching Miss Cook has made it a practice to talk over a class problem with the people most concerned with it—the children. She knows from experience how well they respond to being included in such discussions.

"We have a problem here, children, and I hope you'll be able to help me work it out. *Twelve* people want to work on the bulletin board; *five* of you want to be office monitor; *six* children would like to take care of our library. What would happen if 23 people were doing three jobs?"

The children's reaction is immediate.

"We'd fall over each other at the bulletin board!"

"The principal would be awful mad if five people answered the office bell!"

"The library corner would be pretty noisy with six of us fussing around!"

The humor of the situation strikes them, and teacher and class have a good laugh.

"Well, any ideas?" asks Miss Cook. "Can anyone solve our problem?"

"I'll start," offers Betty. "You can take me off the bulletin board list and put me down for dusting. I don't like to dust, but I'm willing to take my turn." (A scattering of handclaps from the class turns into a real round of applause.)

"I'll work with Betty," says Linda. Then she adds shyly, "May we come up early with you?"

Miss Cook nods agreement.

"I don't like to wash paintbrushes, but I'll help with the art supplies for a month," says Gil.

"We appreciate your offers, children," says their teacher. "When young people are willing to do a job *that has to be done*—even though it may be a bit unpleasant—it's a sign they're growing up. Mother and Dad—even Miss Cook—have to do unpleasant things now and then. How would your home look if Mother did only what she enjoyed? How would your Dad's business succeed if he were unwilling to tackle unpleasant jobs? How would our room look if everyone did only what he likes the most?"

The children get the point. As Miss Cook says, "They have a lot of common sense."

1. In fourth grade your class can begin to keep a daily log of class activities:

    (a) Using volunteers for the first few tries, prepare a chart—one child for each day with the date on which he takes notes.

    (b) The next morning that child will read his log to the class. He will receive suggestions (and possibly criticism) from the class members.

    (c) He rewrites the log and gives it to the class secretary—or a special log secretary—who puts it in a loose-leaf logbook.

    (d) In this way you not only have a running account of *what* happened *when,* but

        (1) It's good composition experience.
        (2) It develops responsibility in the children.
        (3) They show unusual interest in this written account of class trials and accomplishments.
        (4) You can refer to the logbook if you wish to check on a date or a name connected with class activities.

2. In fifth grade—or fourth, depending on your group—try the "leader for the day" idea. Again starting with volunteers, who will give the more hesitant ones the confidence to volunteer later, let your leaders gradually assume these responsibilities (always under your guidance):

    (a) Take charge of opening exercises.
    (b) Help the class plan the day.
    (c) Substitute for an absentee jobholder.
    (d) Assist teacher and classmates when needed.

These ideas work wonders with your class. Children like to feel important, and you'll give them the chance to assume responsibility, assist in planning, and learn to be helpful to others.

A fifth grade chart combining these two ideas might look like this for a week:

Name	Take notes	Read log	Leader for the day
James Matson	Oct. 1	Oct. 2	Oct. 2
Margaret Stone	Oct. 2	Oct. 3	Oct. 3
Esther Jones	Oct. 3	Oct. 4	Oct. 4
Fred Hall	Oct. 4	Oct. 5	Oct. 5
Sam Wade	Oct. 5	Oct. 8 (Mon.)	Oct. 8 (Mon.)

WHAT ABOUT CLASS OFFICERS?

Although fourth grade classes often elect officers such as a president and secretary, these children are scarcely capable of carrying out their duties efficiently. In spite of this many teachers are of the opinion that whatever training children receive in responsibility is all to the good and like to give them this opportunity.

By the time children reach the sixth grade they should have developed sufficiently to be able to select class officers for their particular abilities and not simply because of friendly ties or good looks.

ELECTING OFFICERS IN SIXTH GRADE

Mr. London knows that his sixth graders have been electing class officers for two whole years. After a discussion period with the class his suspicions are confirmed—elections are little more than popularity contests. It's time for a change!

THE NEED FOR CLASS OFFICERS

"Do we *need* class officers?" asks Mr. London. "Take the president, for example, is it important that we elect someone to this office?"

"Yes," says Tom, "to help take charge if the teacher's busy with something else."

"We should have someone to represent our class at a meeting," says Marge.

"When we have a class meeting or have a problem to talk over, he can take charge,"—this from Anne.

"Then," says their teacher, "if this person represents the entire class you will have to make a careful choice. What qualifications should such a person have?"

WHAT MAKES A GOOD PRESIDENT?

"In my last school," says John, "we had a class president who—well—anyway, we weren't very proud of him, so we elected another. I know you have to be careful who's chosen."

"What should we look for in a class president?" asks Mr. London. "Should he be the best looking?" (Laughs from the boys.) "Or the smartest?" (Well, maybe.) "What are the most important traits?"

"Must be reliable—"

"Maybe not the smartest, but not dumb, either—"

"We should be proud of this person—"

"Whoever it is must have self-control—"

"Very good," says Mr. London. "Now, most of you are well acquainted with each other for you've been together a long time. I want you to do some thinking tonight. This isn't a question of voting for your best friend. It's a question of finding the best person for the job."

PLANS FOR ELECTION

The next morning, as soon as the preliminary business is out of the way, Mr. London and his class have a talk about the ideas they have come up with overnight. They decide to have a nominating convention where the names of several candidates will be placed before the group. There will be a short speech as each name is presented in which the speaker gives the reason why his candidate should be elected. (These children have watched conventions on TV and have some idea of how such business is handled.)

The speakers agree to meet individually with the teacher to prepare the best possible speech. The class votes to hold the convention the day after tomorrow.

The nominating convention gives rise to so much enthusiasm that Mr. London's class decides to have the convention meet again to nominate a vice-president and a secretary-treasurer. It is generally agreed that the secretary-treasurer will have to be smart because he or she will be writing letters and collecting money.

SIXTH GRADERS CAN HELP THEIR SCHOOL

Children in the sixth grade—and occasionally in the fifth—are often called upon to assist teachers of small children. Here is a perfect opportunity to impress on young folks of a very impressionable age the great privilege that is theirs in being able to help in the smooth running of the school. If children believe anything is a *privilege* they just can't do enough!

Sometimes in the excitement of being needed by others, their own studies—and their own class and teacher—are neglected. It requires guidance and endless patience on the part of the guide if the services rendered by these children are to be of practical value to the school.

When children are assisting us we often feel it would be easier to do the job alone, but this wouldn't train them in responsibility, nor would it give them that good feeling that comes from a job well done. It's important that teachers take time and have patience to train these youngsters.

Suppose that Mrs. Lang found her trusted library assistants playing "Marching to Jerusalem" with the library chairs instead of preparing the room for Class 4–3——

Or Mr. Jeffry came upon his corner guards of the Safety Patrol firing snowballs at each other instead of getting the little tots safely across the street——

Or the teacher on lunch duty sees her hostesses for first grade tables entertaining the boys who just came off their stairway assignments.

We've all had such experiences. The most normal reaction is for the teacher to blow his (or her) top and order such offenders to report back at 3 PM. By the time 3 PM arrives these children will have built up a wall of resentment against the teacher—no matter how much at fault they have been. You'll be sorry and wish you'd handled it better.

Show surprise. Speak softly. Let them see your disappointment. The effect is much more lasting than a bawling out.

If you are asked to recommend some of your boys and girls to help out in the lower grades think carefully before you put your seal of approval upon them. It's not always the class stars that shine the brightest in these areas.

HOW THE GIRLS CAN HELP

Many small children in first and second grades live at such a distance that they must have lunch in school. Teachers on duty in the lunchroom have to give these little ones so much attention that it's difficult to supervise the others. In one school sixth grade girls volunteered to act as "hostesses," each one being responsible for a table of 10 to 12 children. These girls helped open thermos bottles, wiped up spills, comforted the weepers, and arbitrated when necessary. Girls of 11 and 12 have a knack with small children. The overworked teachers wonder how they ever managed without them!

HELPING AS MONITORS OF YOUNGER GRADES

Teachers of the lower grades frequently ask for older girls to act as monitors to meet their small charges at the bus or in the playground. These girls escort the children to their room, help with coats and boots, and stay until the teacher arrives. The teacher may have been on yard or bus duty, or even delayed in traffic, and it saves her from the additional worry about what's happening to her class.

The same monitors call for the classes at noontime and afternoon dismissal and escort them safely to the bus or across the street. They are faithful and devoted to their little charges. It's interesting and rather touching to see the affection that frequently develops between the bigger girls and the little tots.

HELPING IN THE LIBRARY

If there is a separate library room in your school it usually means that one teacher is assigned the extra work of keeping it in order—besides acting as librarian in her "spare" time. It's an endless, repetitious chore requiring an unbelievable amount of time.

Here is an opportunity for sixth grade boys and girls who love being around books to be of real service. They can make themselves useful as library assistants and quickly learn how to put books back in their proper places on the shelves. They check up on overdue books and deliver and collect books from the classrooms. All these chores are important to the smooth functioning of any library—a fact most of us take for granted.

OTHER WAYS TO SERVE

Not every boy or girl would enjoy working in the library, but they may still want to help in some way. Being a member of the Color Guard in the assemblies has charmed more than one child into acceptable behavior—but it must be considered an honor and a privilege, not simply something to keep one from being a problem.

THE IMPORTANCE OF THE SAFETY PATROL

It is an established fact that the School Safety Patrol saves lives. Sixth grade boys are trained to act as crossing guards, and the children are instructed in the classroom to respect their authority and obey orders. In some schools the girls who supervise first and second grades at dismissal time are considered members of the Safety Patrol, too. All such guards must have their teachers' recommendation for it is a position of trust and they're proud of that badge and white belt.

Not all boys make good crossing guards. For health reasons some cannot stay on their posts in all weathers. Others are not dependable. Those who are selected have to be supervised, for the boys are only human and will horse around instead of doing their job. It's usually a man teacher who gets the assignment of training and supervising the Safety Patrol—and here's another hard, tiring, thankless chore requiring endless supervision and training. (I remember one of our women teachers who was stuck with the job— and did she spruce up that Safety Patrol! The boys practically saluted her as she walked her beat!)

There is a way in which dependable boys, who can't be on the Safety Patrol for one reason or another, can help the school. There's no badge or white belt but it's considered a choice position.

HELPING WITH VISUAL AIDS

Almost as enviable as the boys on the Patrol are the monitors who assist the teacher responsible for visual aids. It's a thrill to sit in the projection booth while classmates remain in assembly seats. Wheeling the various machines into lower grade classrooms and setting up the equipment makes one feel pretty important. Here, too, it's a question of selecting responsible boys and training and supervising them. The equipment is expensive. The teacher in charge of visual aids must familiarize the monitors with the operation and transportation of the machines, arrange schedules for classes, send for material—there is *no simple extra job* assigned to teachers.

FIRST CHECK WITH YOUR SUPERVISOR ABOUT THE USE OF MONITORS

If you are new to the district or a newcomer to town be very sure that you confer with your supervisor about the use of monitors. In many cases you will be encouraged to train young assistants. In other cases there may be regulations limiting this—indeed, even forbidding it.

More and more we find parent volunteers—or paid aids—who take over some of the teachers' burdens. You might inquire about the possibility of children assisting a parent in the lunchroom, yard, or at bus pickups.

Today's children lack the feeling of being needed—of being permitted to help run something. You can see them glow with pride when they have certain duties to perform. Find out what responsibilities they may assume—with supervision, of course—and give them every possible opportunity to serve the school.

SOME SUGGESTIONS THAT WILL MAKE YOUR OWN WORK EASIER

✔ *Get your desk organized*

There is nothing more frustrating and time-consuming than not being able to lay your hands on things! We've all had this experience—"It was here a minute ago. Someone must have taken it!" You know very well that nobody took it because nothing but a pack rat could have found it. How long would it take to fix up that desk and put it in working order?

Use this as your guide—if a substitute teacher were here tomorrow would she be able to find the material needed to do a satisfactory job? Since most teachers' desks are built on the same plan let's take them drawer by drawer. That drawer over the kneehole—keep your plan book there, the roll book, any reports on which you're working, the record book, a ruler, and a pen. Many principals insist that this drawer be kept locked so have *one* place for your keys. In the top right hand drawer have some sharp pencils, a pen or two, and several colored pencils near the front. Some of the articles you need less frequently, such as a stamp pad and a stapler, can be placed further back. If your desk has a deep drawer with movable sections you're lucky, for the modern report cards and records cards will take every inch of it.

On top of the desk keep a large blotter—as fancy as you wish, but large—and a pen that works. Have a good, soft pencil or two, an eraser, and a pair of bookends to hold the textbooks with which you're working at present. For years I have kept an "incoming and outgoing" box on my desk for marked and unmarked papers. It is well worth the room it takes.

✔ *Have a filing system*

Mrs. Wendell is a paragon of tidiness. When she came to our school she measured the space in the closets, brought large cartons from the chain store and used them for filing cabinets. Everything that ever happened in the school, every meeting we ever attended, every circular we ever received was at her fingertips in those files— and they were neat too. Most of us would be physically and mentally incapable of competing with her in this field, *but some kind of filing system is necessary.*

Think of the pictures you collect for social studies units, magazine and newspaper articles, material for special days and seasons. Have you ever had the annoying experience of hunting desperately for a certain Thanksgiving play and finding it when Christmas vacation is over? The file needn't be fancy nor does the system have to be complicated. Use large envelopes for pictures—and label them. Keep posters or large outline maps in mailing tubes—and label them. It will give you great satisfaction if you can put your hands on important material, and you don't have to go and borrow what you need.

✔ *Make a promise to yourself in writing*

Now that you have organized your class, your room, your desk and files, wouldn't it be wonderful to be able to keep things going smoothly all year? There are some events over which you have no control, but you can see that your class regulations are observed; you are training your monitors and officers to do their jobs. *What about yourself?* Can you keep things in place so that you can find them? Can you continue to enjoy the order and convenience so dearly won?

Here is the technique that William E. Edwards in his recent book *Ten Days to a Great New Life* * has given to thousands of people:

1. Make a promise to yourself.
2. Write down that promise
3. Carry it out for 10 days.

Don't think that a promise to maintain the order of your desk is too simple a demand to make of yourself. Try it for 10 days. Keep the written promise where you will see it. You will find it hard, but stick to it. The satisfaction will be enormous and you'll be ready to make another promise to yourself.

To quote Mr. Edwards again, "This promise technique—even when you use it in little things—changes everything fast—brings a new surge of self-reliance—proves to the self that it can count on the self—and that is the heart of the matter."

Amiel, in his journal (1859), says, "Order is man's greatest need, and his true well-being."

———— SOME POINTS TO REMEMBER ————

As soon as the school year begins set up your routines so well that your new class responds to them automatically.

First graders have many routines to learn and the teacher must repeat endlessly and patiently until the children have mastered the most important of them.

If any class, no matter what the grade, is unfamiliar with an important routine, teach it to them at once.

Children of grades 4–6 can perform simple jobs that help in the physical upkeep of the classroom.

---

* *Ten Days to a Great New Life* by William E. Edwards, published by Prentice-Hall.

Fifth and sixth grade children like to elect class officers. Guide them in the selection of the most capable people for the positions.

Children of grades 4–6 enjoy working on a committee. *They need the teacher's guidance* as they work and plan together.

Sixth graders can serve their school by acting as lunchroom and library monitors, or by working with the Safety Patrol, or assisting in the operation of visual aids equipment. Before assigning responsibility to children check with your supervisor to make sure such procedures are permitted.

Make your own work easier by organizing your desk and by keeping some kind of orderly file.

Chapter Three

Planning Your Work

Careful planning is an integral part of teaching and your effectiveness as a teacher depends largely on your willingness to spend the necessary time and effort in this vital preparation.

In order to plan successfully you must be familiar with the general curriculum and have at least a nodding acquaintaince with the entire program of elementary education. You should know what your new class was taught in the previous grades, what will be expected of it in the next grade, and, most important of all, what you will teach it this year.

These children will be with you for a long time. You'll be expected to produce results. It calls for sound planning right down the line.

USE THE SYLLABI PROVIDED FOR YOU

Boards of Education usually provide their teachers with a syllabus for each subject in the curriculum. Every few years these syllabi are updated and the new ideas explained. Any new booklet seems to arrive at an inopportune moment and too often we place it on a shelf or in a drawer "just for now," meaning full well to take it home and read it. There comes a day when that syllabus is needed for our own planning or for a grade meeting, and then we realize how the pile of unread manuals has grown!

Ideally, each one should be read when received and the new facts and ideas checked and noted for future reference. There is one small factor called "TIME" that enters the picture and makes it hard to keep up with all the new material.

If you are new at the job or if you have been lax in your reading for one reason or another, this is the time to start. Take the syllabus you feel you need most—is it art? Music? What about the new developments in math? Science? Make a promise to yourself to read it in a specified length of time. (Here is our promise technique in action again!) Mark it up generously, dog-ear certain pages and make a note of the suggestions you plan to use. These courses of study have some excellent ideas, and even if the printing date is a year or two old the ideas may possibly be better than those you have been using.

LONG-RANGE PLANS FOR YOUR CLASS

Long-range, overall plans are blocked out first. I use some of the extra pages in the back of my plan book for this and they are easily available for reference. These pages can be a strong, central prop for your whole year's work.

    1. List your main areas, such as social studies, math, language arts, science, and so on.
    2. Then put down what you hope to accomplish in each.

IDEAS FOR "PRIMING THE PUMP"

On another page write down *every* way you can think of in which the areas you just listed can be integrated. Some of your thoughts may seem very traditional but don't disdain them for that reason. Some of the thoughts may be new. This technique "primes the pump" and will give rise to more ideas for the integration of subject areas.

Be sure to write down any idea that pops into your mind. You may not find them all useful but it starts ideas coming through, some now, some tomorrow, some next month. Add them to your original list. You will consciously or unconsciously lean on this list, and it will give you a vital, energizing core for organizing a whole year of successful work.

Never, in any grade, feel that you *must* integrate all subject areas. Those that fit naturally together should be taught that way. But now and then there will be something coming up which must be taught separately, on its own, apart from your main project or unit or center of interest. Teach it, and don't worry about its integration.

Relating one subject area to another (or integrating them) is the *natural* way to teach children. Effective teachers have always done this even though it was not always encouraged by old curriculum bulletins (now, fortunately, on the scrap heap).

Take the example of the history and geography of our own country. They are inseparable. Attempting to teach one without relating it to the other would miss the whole point of how geography makes history.

✔ How could we learn about General Wolfe's capture of Quebec without an examination of the situation of that city high on the cliffs above the St. Lawrence River?

✔ And what of the plan of the British generals during the American Revolution to separate the struggling colonies by marching one army across from Lake Erie, to meet a second army coming down from Canada through the Hudson Valley, where they would combine their strength with a third army heading up from New York City? (How delighted the children are when they discover that the plan failed!)

✔ And how, without a knowledge of the geography of the area, could we appreciate the ruthless but exciting march of General Sherman through Georgia to further split a Confederacy already weakened by the loss of the Mississippi River?

The skillful integrating of subject areas is a constant challenge to teachers. When a new idea pops up seemingly out of nowhere, jot it down on anything handy before you forget it and add it to that pump-priming list at your first opportunity.

IDEAS FOR INTEGRATING SUBJECT AREAS

First and second grade units of work center for the most part around the problem of how we live and work together at home with the family and at school with teacher and classmates. The teacher plans ways in which she can integrate the various subjects that are part of this project. (It is somewhat harder in lower grades because the children have few skills. The teacher's planning must take that into account.)

One first grade teacher combined *language arts, science, safety,* and *art* in a visit to the boiler room to talk with the custodian about how he takes care of the school building. The children talked over where they would go and how they would get there, but were curious about what they would find when they arrived at the boiler room.

1. They *kept to the right* on the way through the hall. (Safety)
2. *Held the stair railing tightly—took one step at a time.* (Safety)
3. *Asked the custodian questions* about how he cared for the building. (Language)
4. *Listened while he explained* how the boiler works. (Language) (Science)
5. Watched as he *turned some impressive wheels* to illustrate a point. (Science)
6. *Returned safely* and *dictated* a few salient points to the teacher. (Safety) (Language)

Results: The teacher printed headings on drawing paper, such as:

WE WENT TO SEE THE BOILER ROOM
MR. MILLER WAS WAITING FOR US
WE SAW THE BIG BOILERS
THE BOILERS KEEP US WARM
MR. MILLER TURNED SOME BIG WHEELS
JOHNNY, THE CAT, LIVES IN THE BOILER ROOM

The children drew pictures to illustrate the headings. Then they prepared a little book with its own table of contents—with the help, of course, of the teacher.

A simple little project, but it combined several areas of learning quite neatly.

THIRD AND FOURTH GRADES ENLARGE THEIR WORLD

Children in the third and fourth grades move from the study of home, family, and school to the community—town or city. Now they learn something of local government—the mayor's name, a visit to City Hall, conversations with policemen and firemen about the importance of their work. They study how people live in a

farming community and how they lived there long ago; how people
live in a cold country or on a tropical island.

Let's see how we integrate some of our areas of study in these
grades.

1. Social studies: How old is our town? How did people
live here 50 years ago? 100 years ago? How did they travel?
What tools did they use?

2. Science: Plant life in the city and in the country.
Different types of animals found in cold and warm lands
(camouflage, nature's protective device). Machines used now,
and long ago, in town and in farming communities.

How did people get a supply of water long ago? Where
do we get our water supply? Visit to town or city pumping
station.

3. Health and safety: Fire and police protection in our
town or city. What was it like 50 or 100 years ago? Visit to
firehouse.

How is our water supply kept pure? Bring in pictures and
newspaper clippings for bulletin board display on water
and air pollution.

4. Math: Visit a local market to buy supplies for a class
party.

Money used in the old days (your bank may have an exhibit; a child may have a coin collection).

Barter and trading long ago.

Money used in cold or warm countries.

5. Language arts: Write a class play showing how early
settlers of your town bartered or traded with the Indians for
corn.

BROADER HORIZONS IN FIFTH GRADE

When we come to our fifth graders we find them concerned
with the beginnings and growth of the United States. They become
acquainted with the geography of their land as they move farther
and farther west by canal boat, flatboat, or wagon. Ways of travel;
the constant problem of finding food, water, and clothing; Indian
life; countless heroes—your biggest problem in integrating here
may be trying to include everything. Don't try to! Concentrate on
the high spots of our country's expansion. You can get bogged
down if you try to study too many heroes or too many battles.

THE OUTLINE MAP

I have found the outline map to be an invaluable aid. For years I have had two large black and white wall maps—one an outline may of the western hemisphere, the other of the United States. They have been erased and washed within an inch of their lives. You may use individual outline maps too—they're available in sets of 50 to 100. You can use the large wall map while the children work with individual maps.

If there is no such thing in your supply closet as a black and white outline map, make your own. It's easy, and you get a good deal of satisfaction from the do-it-yourself project. How? Use the opaque projector (see Chapter 6) to make as many large outline maps as you wish. If you do this you'll be able to save your maps for a review or an exhibit.

HOW FIFTH GRADERS CAN USE OUTLINE MAPS

1. When you begin your study of exploration use a political type of world map to start the discussion rolling. The children should have an idea of what countries were involved and what routes were taken.

2. Introduce the outline map of the western hemisphere. Trace the wanderings of the explorers up and down the coastline. The utter *emptiness* of the map impresses upon your class the fact that this was a completely unknown and undiscovered world.

3. Locate any settlement that was started.

4. *Plan a key* for your outline maps—one color for Spanish, another for English, a third for Portuguese, etc. If an explorer made more than one voyage to America trace his routes with a variety of lines, such as:

First voyage _____

Second voyage _____

The ability to use a key (or legend) is an important skill, and if the children learn to make and use their own they will follow through when they come across a more elaborate key in their textbooks.

5. The next map will show colonies established by several European countries. The legend (or key) to the map will show who settled what.

6. Most of your interest will be centered now in North America. As the need arises put in mountains, rivers, lakes. When a child locates the position of a river or a chain of mountains on his own outline map he is much more likely to know where to find it on a complicated, modern political map.

7. When westward migration starts, even prerevolutionary migration, the outline map of the United States will serve your purposes better since it will give you a larger map to work with. Now more rivers are to be added to the map, perhaps more mountains. But keep your color key the same for it's interesting to watch how one color decreases as another grows.

INTEGRATING FIFTH GRADE SOCIAL STUDIES WITH OTHER AREAS

1. **Science:** Thoughtless waste of our forests, wildlife, and topsoil by early settlers and later by westward expansion.

Differences in climate and crops grown caused rapid growth of slavery in the South but not in the North.

Developments in communication sped growth of the nation.

People and events connected with building of canals, railroads, and telegraph lines.

2. **Music:** Songs of early settlers and of pioneers in the West.

First musical instruments brought to America.

Negro spirituals.

How our patriotic songs came to be written.

3. **Art:** Models of early ships, covered wagons, first steamboats, steam engines.

Make bonnets and aprons for a pioneer play.

Paint murals depicting several periods of American history.

4. **Language arts:** There is scarcely another period of time that invites the use of poetry, playwriting—even plain compositions—to the extent that the growth of America does. Its vitality and excitement are very real to a ten-year-old.

SIXTH GRADE HORIZONS ARE WORLDWIDE

The sixth grade takes another giant step when children study this country in relation to the other Americas. They investigate ways in which we are alike and how we differ from our neighbors.

From there they travel abroad to find out what the rest of the world is like, and how we must live in it while we help create better conditions for more people and closer, friendlier ties.

IDEAS FOR INTEGRATION OF SIXTH GRADE AREAS

1. **Social studies:** Watch the UN in action on TV. Become familiar with various personalities such as our own ambassador, the secretary of the UN. Look into the way in which speeches are translated for the mixed racial audience. What is UNICEF? Can we help it?

Read and discuss the *Junior Red Cross Magazine*.

Have a pen pal in a foreign land.

2. **Language arts:** Prepare a class book of original poems and stories about people in foreign lands. The class will prepare a table of contents and an index. This book can be illustrated and bound and donated to the school library.

3. **Math:** Exhibition of coins from other lands and the study of their value in U.S. money.

Ask the local bank to explain as simply as possible the principle of foreign exchange.

4. **Science:** How our country has supplied food for backward areas of the world. The effort being made to train countries to grow their own food, improve the soil and prevent recurrent famine.

Watching the race for space between nations and the effect it has on the relations of the U.S. and other countries.

5. **Physical activities:** Learn dances from such countries as Israel, Italy, and Mexico for Spring Festival.

Make a scrapbook of clippings about international competitions in skiing, swimming, running. If any Olympic games are in progress follow the successes or failures of favorites. How do these athletes train?

PUTTING LONG-RANGE PLANS TO WORK

Long-range planning of the content of your studies and their integration is vital to the success of the year's work. But we must now get down to earth in the week-by-week and day-by-day planning.

There is so much variety in types of weekly plans required by principals and other supervisors that there would be little purpose in discussing the form one should adopt. The content is the important thing. Teachers of long experience may object to spending so much time thinking about and writing up a plan every week. In my own opinion no two classes of children are alike. No matter how many years you have taught the same grade you still need a plan book. New ideas, new procedures, are necessary for each new group.

And what if a substitute teacher is called upon to carry on in an emergency? Your plans will mean a great deal to her. Why object, anyway? Save your strength for writing up your plan book—it has to be done!

THE OLD "PROGRAM CARD"

Some years ago teachers were bound to a cut-and-dried program. At the beginning of the school year you sent a "program card" to the office on which you printed exactly what you would be doing every minute of the day. There was no flexibility permitted. Some teachers objected to dropping an interesting lesson just because "it is 10:20 and at 10:15 you should have started math."

A principal once stopped at my door, looked at the duplicate program card thumbtacked there, checked the hall clock and remarked caustically that I seemed to be teaching social studies when the card indicated that I was 20 minutes late with my spelling lesson. A more imaginative person would have observed that the class was head over heels in a discussion of injustices practiced on the Indians by the pioneers.

THE TIME ELEMENT IN YOUR OWN PLANS

Fortunately for teachers and pupils alike, much more flexibility is permitted now—and in some cases it is even encouraged. But, much as we want this, there are parts of our weekly plans that are bound by definite time limits. These must be taken care of first, and then you can proceed with the more flexible parts of your planning.

SOME OF THE "MUSTS" YOU MAY HAVE TO MEET IN YOUR SCHOOL

Radio and TV programs: If your school is equipped with with a loudspeaker in every room (a mixed blessing) you're going to get certain educational programs whether or not you want them, so put them in the weekly plan with the time allotment for each. TV programs also come on at definite times.

Gym: Probably your whole grade uses the gym three or four times a week. As this place is in demand you have to use it at a specified time.

Assemblies: Two hundred or more children are going to the assembly hall at a certain time. Don't be late. It's embarrassing!

Visual aids: The teacher in charge of visual aids will have the young assistants set up the equipment at a definite time for each class or grade as the arrangement may be. *Plan for this period!* If you're not going to need the equipment on that particular day let the teacher in charge know in advance.

Library: The same holds true of periods in the library. Let the teacher-librarian know ahead of time if you will not be using the room. You may save her and her monitors a good deal of trouble.

If there are any other "musts" in your school, plan time for them—then you can turn to the other subjects.

THE MORE FLEXIBLE PARTS OF YOUR PROGRAM

When planning the rest of your program allow as nearly as possible for the percentage of time suggested by the curriculum bulletin. *Language arts* in any of the elementary grades are given about 30 per cent of the allotment. If this seems a great deal, stop to consider the variety included under the title "Language Arts." Perhaps one of the radio or TV programs listed under "musts" will introduce a certain children's classic which is part of your reading plans for the class. *Discussion* is an important language art and discussions with the children may vary from a disagreement over the way to cross a street (Health and Safety) to the planning of a dramatization for Open School Day. In each case the teacher guides the class in the social graces of listening courteously and speaking clearly. These too are language arts.

THE FLEXIBILITY OF MATH

Math is another subject that fits in well. Take music, for example. From the time kindergarten tots join their first rhythm band to the day sixth graders put one of their original poems to music, math and music are partners.

Think of the inseparability of math and science! Whether the first graders have to know how deeply to plant the crocus bulbs, or the fifth graders try to figure the distance from here to a star, it's math all the way. One of our teachers is fond of saying to the children, "You can't get away from math. If you dig a hole, jump into it, and pull the hole in after you, just turn around and you'll find math right in there with you!" This little illustration amuses the class at first, but soon some of the math buffs (junior size) begin to question the truth of the statement. Then the teacher throws the challenge to the class. "There's math in everything we do. David thinks we're wrong." A lively discussion usually follows. This teacher maintains that even children who care little for math become involved in trying to prove or disprove the truth of the statement.

One thing is sure—math fits into a program anywhere you care to use it.

Another flexible study is *art*. If roughly 10 per cent of your time is to be allotted to it, that time may be used on one day as an hour period for painting if you need an hour to do a satisfactory job. On another day it may become part of a reading lesson when the children make the acquaintance of Michelangelo.

Keeping your program flexible and still giving the various areas their approximate time allotments takes planning—but it's worth it!

DAILY PLANS

As we read in Chapter Two, children enjoy helping to plan the day with their teacher—in a very limited way in lower grades and more actively by the time they reach fourth grade. As early in the new school year as possible have the children copy their class program in their notebooks. In this way a child knows what's on the schedule (when to bring sneakers for gym or wear a white blouse for assembly).

HOW TO GET A JUMP ON THE DAY

Getting the day off to a good start can be a problem; buses bring many pupils from a distance and, like it or not, they sometimes straggle in.

Just as soon as your first arrivals put away coats and boots, start to plan the day with them. They become familiar with this routine, and as soon as they see you at the board with a piece of chalk they know what is expected of them. It quiets the hubbub and gets your class working together. As stragglers come in they tend to join in the planning without any fuss.

List the day's expected activities first (gym, radio or TV programs, etc.) and let the children refer to their individual copies of the program as you plan. Then put in the "flexibles." These can be arranged to suit the convenience of teacher and class—social studies reports, a quiz, art, a rehearsal. At first you will find yourself making most of the plans, but gradually the class will feel more confident in making suggestions. You will always have to be more or less in charge of this planning, but there will come a time when the "leader for the day" will be quite capable of guiding the class in making the daily plan of work.

Children in the fourth, fifth, and sixth grades enjoy it. It creates a feeling of partnership and shared responsibility—important factors in their training.

SAMPLES OF DAILY BLACKBOARD PLANS

In the following samples of daily plans made by teacher and children you will notice how very simply the second grade plans its day. The teacher prints on the board as she guides her class in their plans. Fourth grade takes a long step forward, and sixth grade can operate with a suggestion or two from the teacher—who in each case supervises the planning.

Class 2–2 *Friday, Nov. 3*	*Class 4–1* *Friday, Nov. 3*	*Class 6–3* *Friday, Nov. 3*
Flag salute	Opening exercises	Leader today—Larry
Morning inspection	Health inspection	Health inspection
Reading to the teacher from our library books	Log—Joseph Math—Measures of length	Opening exercises and log—Larry Math—percentages
Games	Game—what's my	TV—short discussion
Math—our store	name?	before and after
Recess	Radio—story time	science program on
Science—how can we make our science corner more inter- esting?	Social studies reports— life on a farm 100 years ago—Ethel; modern farming— Peter	phases of the moon Gym—team practice— basketball throw Social studies— Research in library
	Gym—practice dances for Open School Day	

Class 2–2 *Friday, Nov. 3*	*Class 4–1* *Friday, Nov. 3*	*Class 6–3* *Friday, Nov. 3*
LUNCH	LUNCH	LUNCH
Music—practice songs for Open School Day Social studies—visit to the lunchroom kitchen Painting—what did I see in the kitchen?	Language—dramatize today's radio story Spelling—new words from today's reports Assembly—music practice	Assembly—rehearse Open School Day program Language—test on week's spelling—also synonyms and antonyms

CAN FIRST GRADERS PLAN ANY OF THEIR DAILY ACTIVITIES?

A few years ago I was taking an in-service course at a school some distance from my own. Upon arriving there I was informed that the usual meeting room was being painted and was directed to a first grade room—slightly uncomfortable for adults.

I noticed an arrangement of pictures—cut-outs from magazines—clipped with clothespins and hung across the blackboard. One picture showed a child reading a colorful book, another was of a little girl painting, a third showed a small boy using building blocks to form words. In still another there were children skipping rope and playing ball. Then it dawned upon me that this was the plan the children had made with their teacher—a plan of their own activities of the day. The clothespins permitted the easy shifting of the pictures so that a child could tell at a glance what was coming next.

What a practical, picturesque way to let these tots feel they had a part in the operation of their class!

PLANNING WITH OTHERS ON THE SAME GRADE

It's a good idea to talk over your plans with other teachers on the same grade. These conferences are more effective if they are informal. Meet in one of the classrooms. In fairness to all concerned, a conference of three or four teachers should not be held in the teachers' lounge.

If each teacher on the grade is familiar with what the others are trying to accomplish, arrangements can be made for sharing material such as a limited number of choice research books or a common file of pictures. You may want to plan a joint assembly program or even a play. You can plan for interclass visits, or invite a special guest to talk to the combined classes. (Be sure to get the OK of your supervisor for the last item.)

TEACHERS DEVELOP PROJECTS IN A VARIETY OF WAYS

If there are two or more classes on the same grade, it would be unrealistic to suppose that each teacher might develop a similar project in the same way—nor would we want that to happen. In the first place, each will approach the problem with his own ideas; second, the ability of the children in their classes might vary greatly, as would their interests, and these must be taken into account. When each class completes the project in the way it sees fit you will have far more interesting exchange when it's time for interclass visits.

When you plan a joint assembly program as the culmination of these efforts you'll have a good show with each group making a different contribution. In a Pan-American program, for example, let 6–1 write the script, 6–2 paint the scenery and do the necessary sewing (or perhaps carpentry work), 6–3 prepare the mimeographed programs. All classes join in the dances, and the best voices from the three classes can be trained for the singing.

We have tried this idea in our school and the results have been most gratifying. Teachers enjoy working together. We spend so much of our time working exclusively with children that it warps our point of view. It is refreshing for teachers to share ideas and cooperate in such joint projects.

MORE BONUSES FROM GROUP PLANNING

Here are some of the more unusual ideas that were suggested at these informal conferences. We have tried all of them and found them wonderful:

1. A mother who had taught folk dancing in a middle European country volunteered to teach folk dancing to the whole sixth grade. She did a first-rate job and the children danced as they never danced for us.

2. A father in the stamp business acted as advisor to a newly formed Stamp Club. He was an expert, and the children in the club learned more about stamps than we teachers could have told them.

3. A group of mothers volunteered to assist our over-

worked teacher-librarian by preparing a reference file of pictures to be used by all classes.

4. A list was compiled of mothers who would accompany classes on field trips. This was made available to all teachers.

5. Teachers of several grades met with the teacher in charge of the Safety Patrol to draw up a code for patrol members to follow in dealing with small children.

One of the most exciting events was an invitation to a father, who is an internationally known pianist, asking him if he would play for our school. He accepted graciously and gave a never-to-be-forgotten performance for the entire student body.

UNITS OF WORK

A unit of work should be short and timely when it is planned for small children. One of the first grade favorites is a study of the circus. If it is possible, plan your activity to coincide with the visit of the circus to your town or city. If this isn't practical you may have the acts presented to you on television programs or on film.

After the children have seen some of the acts performed live at the circus or on TV, let them talk about it. They'll be excited. The children will definitely want a circus of their own. Listen and watch so you will have an idea of how many want to be "lions," or "clowns," or "tightrope walkers."

IDEAS FOR INTEGRATING SEVERAL AREAS IN THE STUDY OF THE CIRCUS

The diagram on Page 45 shows at a glance how easily our circus fits into other areas of the curriculum.

CHILDREN LOVE ACTION

• Your "lions" escape and the brave lion tamer brings them back.

• The tightrope walkers demonstrate their skill (on a chalk line) and invite the spectators to join them.

FLEXIBLE PLANNING PERMITS THE UNEXPECTED TO HAPPEN

Sometimes one short unit of work leads directly to another. I recall a first grade class that had just about finished their circus

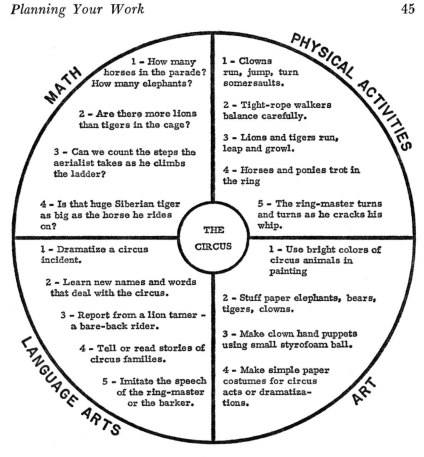

1 - How many horses in the parade? How many elephants?

2 - Are there more lions than tigers in the cage?

3 - Can we count the steps the aerialist takes as he climbs the ladder?

4 - Is that huge Siberian tiger as big as the horse he rides on?

MATH

1 - Clowns run, jump, turn somersaults.

2 - Tight-rope walkers balance carefully.

3 - Lions and tigers run, leap and growl.

4 - Horses and ponies trot in the ring

5 - The ring-master turns and turns as he cracks his whip.

PHYSICAL ACTIVITIES

THE CIRCUS

1 - Dramatize a circus incident.

2 - Learn new names and words that deal with the circus.

3 - Report from a lion tamer - a bare-back rider.

4 - Tell or read stories of circus families.

5 - Imitate the speech of the ring-master or the barker.

LANGUAGE ARTS

1 - Use bright colors of circus animals in painting

2 - Stuff paper elephants, bears, tigers, clowns.

3 - Make clown hand puppets using small styrofoam ball.

4 - Make simple paper costumes for circus acts or dramatizations.

ART

activities when they saw on television the way in which the animals were being moved from one city to another. Before the teacher quite realized what was happening she and the children were involved in the study of how people travel. It had not been planned that way, but the teacher was smart enough to see the interest in this new subject and make good use of it—even though the long-range plans had not called for such an activity.

Keep your plans flexible so that you and your class will not miss some of the enjoyable unexpected's. When the children show special interest in a topic that you had not considered in your long-range plans it is often worthwhile to take the time to capitalize on their interest. As in the above illustration it may not take long, perhaps only a few days or a week. It is also possible that it will mushroom into a project that your class will long remember.

INTEREST SHOWS THROUGH

When we are dealing with a subject in which children are vitally interested, and don't have to battle for their attention, there is almost no end to what we can accomplish with them.

WHAT CAN HAPPEN WHEN A CLASS GETS EXCITED ABOUT SOMETHING REAL

One of the most satisfying years I ever experienced as a teacher was spent with a fifth grade class in a Long Island suburban town. These children had acquired the reputation of becoming easily bored unless they were constantly challenged by new activities.

We started out peacefully enough. They loved to read, enjoyed doing research, and kept the room bright with illustrated book report covers, paintings, and models of explorers' ships—all very conventional. But I was conscious of a sort of simmering, a potential waiting to be used.

When we studied the persecution of religious groups in England and the consequent migrations to America I could see their interest was normal. Normal, that is, until we came to George Fox and the Quakers. Something about these kind, simple people caught the fancy and imagination of the class.

JOHN BOWNE AND THE BOWNE HOUSE

I told the children the story of John Bowne, an Englishman, who brought his wife, Hannah, to America and settled in the little Dutch colony of New Netherlands. In 1661 John and Hannah built a small home in Flushing, Long Island, with a fireplace "big enough to roast a whole ox." Hannah became a Quaker and then the lives of this simple couple changed. In spite of Peter Stuyvesant's decree outlawing the "disobedient" Quakers, Hannah and John invited the persecuted group to meet in their little home. George Fox, and William Penn, too, preached to the Quakers gathered there. John Bowne went to jail for his kindness.

HOW INTEREST CAN MOUNT

When the children realized that the old Bowne House is still standing and can be visited they voted unanimously to hire a bus and see it for themselves. The good ladies of the Fushing Historical Society were contacted and a date arranged.

Our well-informed guide was waiting for us and had a cheerful fire burning in the famous fireplace. She just happened to mention that The Flushing Remonstrance had been signed in the very room in which we were gathered and added that The Flushing Historical Society was at that time trying to have a commemorative stamp made to honor the anniversary of the document and they hoped it would picture the Bowne House.

Then a flood of questions started:

> What was The Flushing Remonstrance? (A document signed by the people of Flushing demanding religious liberty for all.)
>
> Weren't the people afraid of Stuyvesant? (Yes! Some of them were put in jail.)
>
> Will you get the commemorative stamp? (We hope so, but there is so much to be done, and we need help.)
>
> Can we help? (Yes, indeed.)

That did it! Now the children had their teeth in something that challenged them. Each challenge met and overcome led to another. Some of the challenges seemed formidable, but never at any time did they want to quit. The details would fill a book. But to make it brief——

> 1. Fortunately we had the enthusiastic backing of the principal. With his help and suggestions we engineered a drive throughout the neighborhood which resulted in a petition of over 4000 signatures. We sent it to the Postmaster General asking for the commemorative stamp.

> 2. A constant stream of letters was sent from the children of the class to principals of local schools, religious leaders of the community, and to our congressman, asking for their support and interest. (All had to be OK'd by our principal.) The congressman came and spoke to the assembly.

> 3. In order to awaken the interest of the fourth, fifth, and and sixth grade classes of the school the children wrote plays dramatizing the signing of The Flushing Remonstrance and presented them to the assembly.

> 4. The stamp was issued that December. We did not get our beloved Bowne House pictured on it, but it did honor the signing of The Flushing Remonstrance, and that historic document and a quill pen were displayed on the stamp. We were very proud!

WAS THIS TO BE THE END OF SUCH A PROJECT?

One might think that the children had seen enough of the project by this time. It might have been so were it not for three ambitious youngsters who had an idea.

"Here's all this research we've been doing. Here are plays, poems, compositions, drawings, paintings, blocks of stamps. Let's do something with them."

And we did. We made them into a book and typed it, and indexed it, and bound it, and put it on display in the glass exhibit case outside the office door. The blocks of stamps, first date of issue envelopes, and newspaper accounts of our efforts were placed with the book, and we christened the exhibit "A STAMP IS BORN."

A COMPLETE INTEGRATION OF SUBJECT MATTER

Every subject in the curriculum, and most of the skills the children had ever learned, were integrated in this activity. The project grew of itself and new challenges had to be met each step of the way. Enthusiasm never faltered. There was interest and excitement and a sense of achievement throughout.

CAN ANY CLASS ACCOMPLISH AS MUCH?

In the above illustration we have the happy combination of an alert class in need of a challenge and the perfect challenge being presented to them. Not every class would have responded with such enthusiasm, nor would every challenge have presented so many problems to be solved.

However, the basic principles involved are the same. *Start with something the children know and build from there.* You have to be familiar with the group with which you're working. To some a challenge is an awakening; to others a similar challenge might fall flat, or prove too much and end in discouragement. Actually, the teacher's judgment has to be the guideline. Just be sure you don't underestimate the capabilities of your class. Have you ever *really challenged* them?

— POINTERS FOR EFFECTIVE PLANNING —

Careful planning is essential to good teaching.

Long-range plans should be flexible and made with the year's work in mind.

The *natural* way to teach children is to integrate subject areas. Do not feel that you *must* integrate all subject areas. If something comes along that does not integrate naturally, teach it separately.

Plan with other teachers on the same grade for most gratifying results.

Weekly plans should have flexibility too. However, some periods such as gym and assemblies must be scheduled for a definite time.

Children enjoy helping the teacher put a daily plan of activities on the blackboard.

A unit of work for small children should be timely and usually of short duration.

Older children can sustain interest in a project for a longer period of time. How long depends largely on the teacher's ability to present challenges to the class.

Chapter Four ~

Creating Interest:
Your Major Challenge

$\mathcal{I}$f there is any one skill that makes a teacher effective it's the ability to create interest in the teaching content. Some subjects are inherently interesting, but in most cases the interest must be created. The creation of that interest is the teacher's big job.

There's a basic formula to follow here. The heart of the formula is this: you must find a way to tie in the lesson you're teaching with something the child already knows, something he's already familiar with, something in which he's already interested.

More than 60 years ago William James outlined the formula with brilliant precision. He gave teachers three steps to use in the creation of interest in *anything:*

1. Begin with the line of the child's native interests and offer him objects that have some immediate connection with these.

2. Next, step by step, connect with these first objects and experiences the later objects and ideas which you wish to instill.

3. Associate the new with the old in some natural and telling way, so that the interest being shed along from point to point finally suffuses the entire system of thought.*

Every effective teacher, whether he realizes it or not, is following

---

* William James, *Talks To Teachers*. Longmans Green & Co.

this formula. *You must be able to tie in the lesson to something the child already has.*

James continues to say: ". . . . the difference between an interesting teacher and a tedious teacher is little more than the inventiveness by which the one is able to mediate associations and connections, and in the dullness in discovering such transitions which the other shows."

The "tying-in" technique must be varied to fit the subject and varied to the needs of the children—whether for science, reading, social studies, or math—whether for first grade or sixth—whether for overprivileged or underprivileged.

The interesting, exciting teacher is always on the lookout for some new fact, some new idea, that will serve as the connecting link for creating interest. Everything is "grist to his mill."

Miss Brett, for example, never goes anywhere "without her class," as she puts it. She's always looking for something she can use, whether at the theater, or at a picnic, or at a flower show. She brings back some object from every trip, keeps it handy, and waits for the appropriate moment to bring it into play.

Let's look at some examples of the interest-creating technique in action.

WHEN THE TEXTBOOK IS OUTDATED

Young Mr. Jackson impatiently pushed aside the outdated geography book. The gray heading, "Our Good Neighbor, Canada," stared back at him. Even the picture of a Mountie seemed pale and uninteresting. His sixth graders deserved better than that—not a bright group, but he had seen what they could accomplish when their interest was aroused. From what he had been able to piece together their social studies in fifth grade could have been no more than boring assignments—reading a certain number of pages and mechanically reciting the facts to the teacher. Fifth grade, where children learn to love the whole exciting story of their nation's growth!

MR. JACKSON'S TECHNIQUE

When his class came back after lunch Mr. Jackson greeted them with a grin.

"How would you like to talk about your neighbors?"

He saw his pupils glance at one another questioningly and then smile. They were interested, certainly.

"I have a neighbor," he continued, "who gives a big, noisy party every Saturday night. The music is so loud it disturbs the whole block. His guests bang car doors and race motors at 2 AM. . . ."

Hands were waving all around the room.

"What do you want to tell us, Marie?"

Marie flushes and laughs. "We have a neighbor who has nine kids and . . ."

Joe, Bill, Ellen, and Peter add their hair-raising stories and the class is getting a bit out of hand, but Mr. Jackson knows what to do. He puts up his hand for silence and says quietly, "Now hear this. In my apartment building there is a sweet little old lady whom I do not know very well, but we always speak when we meet. Once when she hadn't seen me for several days she asked the superintendent if I was all right. He told her I was sick, and what do you think she did? She brought me soup, and custard, and shopped for me. She took clothes to the laundry and cleaned my apartment. And she's just a neighbor of mine."

More hands waved, but in a slightly subdued manner.

"When my mother had a baby last winter, and my father had to go to work every day . . . ," and Josie tells of a kind neighbor.

"I broke Mr. Brown's window," begins Sammy, "and I was afraid he'd be awful mad, but . . ."

And the stories of good neighbors continue. While the interest is still at its height Mr. Jackson says, "You have neighbors—I have neighbors. Some are unpleasant, some are kind, and some we scarcely know. Did it ever occur to you that our country has neighbors too—all kinds of neighbors?"

This young teacher's class is ready and anxious to be introduced to their good neighbor, Canada. His imaginative approach to the subject has started the children thinking of Canada with a personal kind of interest.

MRS. LEEDS USES A VERY DIFFERENT TECHNIQUE

Mrs. Leeds is using an entirely different technique to introduce the subject of Canada. She has the assurance of years of experience, but in spite of her long years of teaching she is never bored—or boring—when social studies is the subject at hand. Let's listen in while she introduces Canada to *her* sixth grade boys and girls—a "middle" group in a middle class community. They have been discussing the one o'clock weather bulletin which has forecast a cold wave approaching from Canada in the next 24 hours.

"How does it happen that Canada so frequently sends us a cold wave in winter?" she asks.

The answer seems simple. "Because it's north of us, and in the north it's cold," says Jim with assurance.

"If you were to go to Canada what would you find?" she asks Jim.

"Deep snow, glaciers, icebergs . . ."

"Eskimos?" suggests Anne.

"Ski jumpers," adds Betty.

"They're wrong, Mrs. Leeds," says Ted. "I went to Canada once and I saw apple orchards and I went swimming too."

"What are the people like? How would you describe a Canadian?" asks the teacher.

"They're small and dark, like Eskimos," says one.

"I think they're tall and blond like Vikings," says another.

"They speak French," says a third.

"Some people think Canadians travel in dogsleds," says John with contempt, "but that's not true. I saw a picture of Toronto and there were cars all over."

"I'm sure they dress in fancy costumes," offers Sally, "because my aunt went to Quebec and she mailed a card to me."

INTEREST MOUNTS

"I'm going to surprise you," announces Mrs. Leeds in a mysterious manner. Every eye is on her. *"I am a Canadian!"* (Stunned silence.) "I was born in Canada and lived there as a child. My parents were born there, and my grandparents too."

QUESTIONS FROM AN INTERESTED GROUP

Now the class wants to know—
Are there glaciers and orchards too?
Are there dogsleds and big cities?
Can one go skiing and swimming too?
Are there some short, dark people and tall, fair ones?

Do they speak French? But Mrs. Leeds speaks English. Did her parents speak French?

In fifth grade didn't we study about a war with Canada?

Weren't the French and English fighting each other in Canada?

Mrs. Leeds writes the questions on the board as fast as they come. Finally the entire blackboard is covered and children and teacher sit back to laugh and to catch their breath.

A PROBLEM ARISES IN THIRD GRADE

Let's see how Miss Martin handles a science problem in her third year class. These children are quick and of better than average ability. They have watched with great interest the preparations made before each space shot and breathlessly await the results of cameras sent up to take pictures of the moon. Their art work on exhibit in the classroom shows some fairly good attempts to paint launching pads and space capsules.

All this is fine. The children enjoy talking about and writing little stories about astronauts and possible moon men. Their parents are proud and a little awed by the whole thing. Miss Martin is proud too, but still she feels that her class is missing something that little children should have. How could she make them aware of the "wonder in the near-at-hand," for this is science, too. How many little miracles happen around us all the time—miracles of which so few of us are conscious? There must be some simple way to guide the interest of such a lively group into this channel. And if she succeeded in doing it there'd be no telling how far-reaching it might become.

PETER PROVIDES THE ANSWER

Miss Martin thought about this as she walked back and forth in the playground where the duty schedule had placed her. There was Peter strutting around with a pollynose flattened on his own little pug nose. Mary and Debbie followed him trying to keep their pollynoses in place. And there was Jack, the class rascal, munching an after-lunch apple, out of mischief for the moment.

Miss Martin walked over to the children.

"I would like you to bring those pollynoses back to the room," she said, "and Jack, will you wrap your apple core in this tissue and bring it with you when we go upstairs?"

The children looked at their teacher in wonder (pollynoses in the classroom!, apple cores!) but she just smiled. "Maybe we'll have a surprise for the class."

Of course Jack and the others spread the news, and by the time Miss Martin and the class reached their room some speculation had taken place.

WHAT IS MISS MARTIN'S SURPRISE?

"All right, Peter," said the teacher when the children had quieted down. "You may bring that pollynose of yours up to the front. Yes, Mary and Debbie, brings yours, too. Johnny (to a quiet, thoughtful boy somewhat lost in this lively group) will you please look carefully at one of the pollynoses and tell us what you see?"

Johnny picked up one of the pollynoses and examined it. He picked up another and looked at it closely.

"Some seem to have two wings, Miss Martin, and others have only one. I think I've seen these around maple trees. One has a big seed in it, but the other must have lost it. Can these seeds fly?"

Johnny's quiet observation and question led to a spirited discussion of such fascinating seeds as those of the dandelion that have their own tiny parachutes, and the sticky burrs that you can scarcely pull off your sleeve.

JACK CONTRIBUTES TO THE SURPRISE

Then it was Jack's turn. Under his teacher's guidance he broke open the apple core and spread the seeds on a sheet of white paper for all to see.

"There are little 'rooms' in the core and each one has some seeds," said one.

"But these seeds don't have any wings," said another.

"Let's plant them," suggested Ellen, "and grow our own apples."

"What do apple seeds and maple seeds need to grow?" asked Miss Martin.

"Dirt," "Sun," "Rain," came the answers.

"Suppose we experiment with them," suggested the teacher. "We have plenty of seeds, and some may grow strong, and others may not."

The idea of an experiment—such an important sounding word—appealed to the youngsters.

"Let's plant one in the terrarium," "And one in a window pot," "And one with wings," "And one without wings," came the suggestions thick and fast.

A VERY POPULAR EXPERIMENT

As it turned out, nearly everyone brought in some kind of contribution during the next few days. There were grapefruit and orange seeds, a dandelion, one beautiful avocado seed, lima beans, and some dried marigold seeds that were sent by an interested parent. The sunny window-sill became lined with an array of flowerpots, half-pint milk containers, and juice cans, each bearing the name of the plant, the date of planting, and the owner's name.

Miss Martin's third year classroom became a point of interest for the entire school. As the plants grew, other classes visited and had the whole plan explained to them. The principal brought in visitors who admired the garden and asked interested questions of the proud owners.

A DIFFICULT QUOTATION PRESENTS A CHALLENGE TO CHILDREN

On one red letter day the district superintendent came to admire the class project. He must have been briefed before his visit because he turned to the blackboard and wrote, "I believe a leaf of grass is no less than the journeywork of the stars." * After he discussed and explained the quote to the children it opened up a whole new line of research for these busy, inquisitive third graders.

There has been no loss of interest in our nation's race in space. Each new effort is watched and discussed and applauded. You may see proof of this on the class bulletin board and in their compositions and art work. The new interest in seeds and plants has broadened the horizon of each child. He now sees science as something he can touch and feel, something that's all about him and is very much a part of his life.

HOW TO CREATE INTEREST WITHOUT TEACHING A LESSON

Sometimes you can create interest in a subject without teaching a special lesson. For example, you can create interest in reading by placing an attractive display of books where it is sure to be noticed.

---

* Walt Whitman, "Song of Myself."

Ideally, interest in reading begins in the home. An experienced first grade teacher can tell in a day or two which of her new pupils have come from homes where books are loved and read. These children will gravitate to the library table like birds to a feeding station. They open the books, look at the pictures, and perhaps even pretend to read. They will tell you about the pictures and ask you to read something to them.

But what of the child who comes from a home where there is little interest in books? Or the child who comes from a home where books are for show only, and who has been told repeatedly, "Don't touch!" How can you create in him the interest in books which you want him to have?

MAKE ATTRACTIVE BOOKS EASILY AVAILABLE

Put your most attractive and colorful books in easily available places. It is unnecessary to make any comment or to purposely draw the child's attention to them. Let him have the excitement of discovery. The books will speak for themselves. As he moves about the room he will see one cover with a most unusual bear or perhaps a fascinating cat. A raccoon may be watching him through a black mask, or an interesting family group is enjoying a picnic. Being blessed with curiosity, he is sure to examine one. Let him touch the book, open it, turn pages, study pictures. When he asks you a question your victory is half won.

THE TECHNIQUE IS SIMPLE

Allow your new first graders to feel at home in their classroom. There are, of course, certain do's and don'ts that must be taught. But do permit and encourage them to touch and examine the books—after all, you did put them on display, and you do want the children to enjoy them.

When a child brings a book to you encourage him to talk about a picture or two. What he wants and needs is to share his discovery with you.

Keep a "fun" book with large pictures on your own desk and read it to the class when time permits. Let them discuss the large pictures and the story too as they become familiar with the characters in it. It's a great triumph when they realize that they can "read" the names of some of the favorite storybooks.

Your library corner may have room for just a few shelves. You may even have to use packing cases. With a bit of thought and effort a teacher can make this the most attractive and interesting corner of the room where bright book jackets invite children to pause and examine them.

This holds true all through the elementary grades.

THE TEACHER WHO NEEDED A GREATER VARIETY OF BOOKS

Mr. Walters, a fifth grade teacher, felt that the library books available in his school left much to be desired. This seemed to be especially true of American history. His class liked the colorful illustrations in their history textbook and the information was adequate. However, the children's reports were lackluster and unimaginative and it was evident that they were not using a variety of research material.

This bothered Mr. Walters. He was a history buff from way back and enjoyed telling his classes the thrilling stories of explorers, pioneers, and famous leaders. Some years earlier when his own son had reached the age of 10 the father had subscribed to a series of books on the United States written by outstanding authors of history and biography. He remembered how the boy would wait impatiently for a new volume to arrive each month. The collection had grown to 80 or 90 books.

MR. WALTERS HAS AN INSPIRATION

Suddenly Mr. Walters saw the light. How could he have been so blind! The next morning he added two of these volumes to the library corner knowing well that either Janet or Bill would soon find them. Before all the coats and rubbers were tucked out of sight Bill and Janet were racing each other to their teacher's side.

"Mr. Walters! Look! A book about the Erie Canal! Look, Mr. Walters!—Francis Scott Key! May we take them home? May we?"

NEW BOOKS CREATE NEW INTEREST

Their enthusiasm was contagious and spread like wildfire. Soon Mr. Walters was bringing a new book every week, sometimes two. His son didn't mind. He was now in high school and adopted a philanthropic attitude toward the project. At least four parents, delighted with the blossoming interest in reading, presented their children with a subscription to the series of books.

HOW TO CREATE INTEREST IN ORAL COMMUNICATION

I have found that choral speaking is an excellent way to create interest in oral communication. The children love it. They get a big thrill out of joining with other voices and letting go dramatically as the poem changes in tempo and feeling.

One of the great extra benefits of choral speaking is this: it gets rid of the stage fright that bothers so many children when they must speak before others. They find safety and security in the united effort. It seems to pull the timid ones along in spite of themselves. (Here is another reason why it's so important for a teacher to know how to create interest. *Whenever* interest is created, *whenever* the child gets all wrapped up in something and forgets about himself his self-consciousness is lessened and his timidity along with it.)

You can step up the interest still further by choosing poems for choral speaking that are closely connected with subjects in which the children are already interested—for example, "Casey at the Bat" with its baseball theme, and "Oh Captain, My Captain," whose subject is Abraham Lincoln.

TRY THIS TECHNIQUE

Let's take "Casey at the Bat." * I have found baseball season the best time to introduce this lively bit of literature. Practice your own part in this for *you* will present the poem to the class and it *must* be done right!

There will be many stories the class will want to tell when you have finished your reading or recitation of the poem. In the baseball season feeling runs high in schools. Let them talk about it. Have them read it to you in unison. It may be noisy, but you have much to gain, so forget the noise for the time being. It allows the children to get rid of some pent-up energy.

You have a sudden inspiration! How would you children like to do this for the assembly? Maybe during the World Series? How much time have we to prepare it? It has to be absolutely perfect,

---

* "Casey at the Bat" by Ernest Lawrence Thayer, *San Francisco Examiner*, June 3, 1888.

you know. Who would make a good umpire? Who would be the ideal Casey? And who should be that wonderful "someone in the stands" who has the most exciting five words in the poem?

You notice Elsa, that shy, sad little 10-year-old from a foreign country. Her usually pale cheeks are pink with excitement and she's actually laughing. If only you could persuade her to take that part!

Time to go home. Someone is lingering at the door. It's Elsa, shy, but determined.

"Teacher—do you think—could I be the one—that—yells at the umpire?"

"Of course, Elsa, you'd be perfect for the part!"

All goes well at rehearsals. The great day comes, and it is time to perform. The mighty Casey stands, bat in hand, at one side of the platform—the pompous umpire opposite. The fans who carry the burden of the poem stand in the middle of the stage. As the umpire calls "STR——I–KE ONE–N–N–NE" Elsa rushes to the front brandishing her small fists. "KILL HIM! KILL THE UM——PI——RE!" she shrieks.

The audience is enthusiastic. It cheers and applauds. Can the show go on? Elsa is the heroine of the moment and the talk of the school for the rest of the day. Her classmates are thrilled and tell her, "Good work, Elsa! You sure told that umpire!" The shy child's life opened up at that moment. She had conquered! She had become so interested that she forgot to be afraid. When is teacher planning the next show?

HOW TO CREATE INTEREST IN WRITTEN COMMUNICATION

One form of expression that is generally considered less exciting than reading or speaking is composition, the written language. It requires many skills of a child, and much thought. (1) How often have you heard a class sigh when it is book-report time? (2) And what about the question so often asked upon returning from a wonderful class outing—"Do we _have_ to write about it?"

> 1. Encourage the reading of more and more books and let the children write _short_ reports on them. Don't settle for a _few_ books and _long_ reports that are boring to child and classmates and time-consuming for the teacher.

2. As for the trip—don't spoil it with the threat of a written report to follow. Tell the children in advance that you'll be asking for a paragraph or two (100 to 200 words) about something that happened—something funny, or exciting, a discovery, a new route to the destination, possibly an article for the class news, or even for the school magazine.

If you are teaching fourth, fifth, or even sixth grade you may have pupils who somehow have been lost along the way—seem hopelessly bad at composition and need coaching in the simplest forms of written language. I have used second year techniques to rouse the interest of such children and give them the confidence they have lost or never acquired. I have seen a child in fifth grade so unsure of himself that he feared to put words on paper. And I have seen this very child glow with pride when he succeeded in composing a six-line story about his goldfish. He wanted to start one about his dog right away. His teacher's satisfaction was greater than when a medal was awarded to another class member for the best essay on fire prevention.

TECHNIQUE USED IN SECOND GRADE

As soon as a little child acquires some knowledge of reading he is taught to spell simple words and to write them. In second grade he is encouraged to use this unfolding ability to put his own words on paper in the form of a story.

Let the class talk about some marvelous occurrence—perhaps the guppies in the aquarium have new babies, maybe a long-watched cocoon has opened. Print three or four simple sentences suggested by the children on the board and just watch their eyes brighten!

Repeat this technique for several days using a variety of interesting stories. Ask them if they would like to copy it in their notebooks. (The noteboook is a new experience for most of them and is a source of interest and pride.) Give the class plenty of time, and as you go from desk to desk be generous with your praise and sparing of criticism.

Ask Joey, Jane, and Tim to tell you a story. Put three or four sentences on the board for each child. Lo and behold! Tim can read *five* different words in his story.

YOUNG CHILDREN LEARN HOW TO "PLAN" A STORY

Gradually (and such a technique must be used very gradually with small children) show them how to plan a story so that one thought follows another in an orderly manner. "What shall I write about? What happened? How does my story end?" Don't worry about short sentences. There's a danger that children will run everything together with no punctuation if you insist too soon upon longer sentences.

In third grade the ability to compose a story improves rapidly. Your children enjoy the experience of building new words and want to put their enlarged vocabulary to use. Now a child writes about many topics and as often as possible let him choose his own. If he wants to tell about a book he has read try to refrain from calling it a book report—unless he wants to write a "book report" because that's what his big sister does.

Some popular topics at this age are:

WHAT I WONDER ABOUT
JUST SUPPOSE I HAD ONE HUNDRED DOLLARS
IF I HAD BEEN AN INDIAN
WHEN I AM A FAMOUS STAR
MY DOG, REBEL

These topics are still favorites when children are considerably older than third grade students, but the content of the compositions should be different.

CONTENT OF COMPOSITIONS IMPROVES IN FOURTH GRADE

By the time children reach the fourth grade most of them have become familiar with the basic skills needed for written communication—such skills as spelling and penmanship. Now the teacher faces another problem. Which is more important in written work, content or appearance?

INTEREST VS. APPEARANCE

Miss McKay has the bright group—30 fourth graders who are lively, interested, full of questions. Their oral English lessons are a delight for teacher and pupils. The principal is sure to send student teachers to Miss McKay to observe the manner in which she handles oral reports, an original skit, or a discussion of possible projects for the coming science fair.

But what happens when these young ones try to put their thoughts on paper? Little hands simply cannot keep pace with such busy brains. One child scribbles his way through because he wants to finish his work. Another throws down his pencil in despair. Miss McKay maintains strongly that she never will sacrifice their interest and enthusiasm for a neat paper.

"Neatness will come with experience," she says. "Interest is all-important!"

THE DANGER OF KILLING INTEREST

In the adjoining room Mrs. Allway prides herself on being an old-fashioned teacher. There's no nonsense in *her* room! Book reports, essays, and spelling tests hang in neat rows—not even a misplaced thumbtack on *her* bulletin boards. You walk into the classroom and even the chalk is placed symmetrically. The children are working silently. On the board is a beautifully written outline for a composition on a given subject and the entire class is following it to the letter.

EACH TEACHER FEELS SHE IS RIGHT

Each teacher is confident that she is doing the right thing for her children. The principal opens Miss McKay's door and stays to enjoy the bouncing good spirits in evidence there. He enjoys talking with this class. "They always give me a new slant on something," he laughs. He goes into Mrs. Allway's room and compliments her and the children on the peace and orderliness of the surroundings.

There is no simple answer to such a problem. Written work has to be legible, and Miss McKay's papers are really pretty bad in appearance. Mrs. Allway's compositions are lifeless but beautiful to behold. If we could combine the best of each our problem would be solved. Perhaps neatness and legibility *will* come with experience. The greater amount of written work required in fifth and sixth grades will almost certainly give the children plenty of practice in the necessary basic skills. But we must try to achieve this balance without killing interest.

LIMERICKS ARE FUN

Have you ever tried limericks or nonsense rhymes in upper elementary grades? If you have, you are familiar with the pleasure and relaxation they provide for your class. When the children try writing their own they have some real fun. Try collecting original limericks for a class book that can be illustrated and bound by the children.

Following the same procedure, use original stories for your book. You may make it more attractive by having one committee type the stories and a second committee illustrate—in color, of course.

HOW ONE POEM WAS CREATED

I recall one class, quite average, whose teacher happened to remark to them that the last two answers in a social studies discussion seemed to rhyme. She turned to the board and wrote the sentences in question. The children were fascinated to discover that they could beat out the rhythm. By the time two more lines had been contributed, interest had reached such a peak that all other plans were dropped. When the lunch bell rang, accompanied by groans of disappointment (if you can imagine such a thing!), the class and the teacher had a poem of their own on the board—a poem that compared pioneer travel with modern planes. And were they proud!

When the class returned after lunch they suggested some changes that improved this literary effort. Before three o'clock the poem, their own creation, was considered worthy of being sent to a magazine the children read and enjoyed. The class secretary mailed it on her way home, supervised by a goodly number of her classmates.

This was one of those rare occasions when teacher and class are working together so perfectly that it would be unthinkable to allow another lesson to interfere.

P.S.—THE POEM WAS PUBLISHED!

We have been discussing at some length techniques that will help you arouse the interest of your pupils in various subjects. Lets' turn our attention to math for a moment.

CHILDREN ENJOY MODERN MATH

If you are teaching the new math (as it's still called) you know that children enjoy it. There's little difficulty in gaining their attention or holding their interest. The most general complaint among teachers seems to be that they have had this thrust upon them too suddenly. They must learn a whole new way of thinking and a whole new math language, and when you're teaching a "new language" you think in the familiar tongue and translate as you proceed. In-service courses are helping us keep a step or two ahead of our children, and we're learning. Those who are instructing teachers in the mysteries of modern math tell us that we would never against be satisfied with a traditional teaching program.

BUT WHAT ABOUT NEEDED DRILL?

However, we find that there still must be some basic drill in arithmetic. The utter boredom of such things as writing tables has taken the heart out of many would-be learners. Drill for drill's sake is useless and frustrating. I remember as a child writing table after table for the simple reason that our assignment was to fill the paper with multiplication tables. Perhaps there were a half-dozen facts that I could have drilled on to some purpose. How much better to study a few tricky combinations that give you trouble than to waste time and temper on useless review.

Let's hope the day comes soon when computers can be used to find the individual child's "concept block" and drill him on that until he passes to a new level.

NOT EVERY STEP IN LEARNING CAN BE INTERESTING

There are children who make no attempt to learn the basic procedures in arithmetic. Perhaps they have accepted defeat due to a parent's attitude toward the subject—the "I never liked it either" attitude. Perhaps, sad to say, because of a tired, impatient teacher's sarcasm. I recall one child in a seventh grade class whose teacher remarked to her caustically in front of the class, "Your bump of arithmetic is a dent!" The child was smart enough to know exactly what her teacher meant and she never forgot it. She still uses it for an excuse for her weakness in math.

A SURPRISING TECHNIQUE THAT WORKS

One perfect technique can be used in dealing with the child who shows no interest in math—*arouse his fighting spirit!* Appeal to his fighting instincts; arouse his pugnacity! Here is your "tying-in" technique in action.

"Are you going to let a thing like division get the better of you?"

"Are you willing to let this problem in measures throw you for a loss?"

"Where's your pride?"

Impress him with the fact that a few things *can't* be made interesting but still must be learned. Real people can do an uninteresting thing just because it *has to be done.* To believe that everything should be made easy is "kindergarten stuff"—and he certainly is not a baby!

This is not the traditional way of creating interest, *but it works.*

—— HIGH POINTS IN THE CREATING OF —— INTEREST

The ability to create interest in a subject is the effective teacher's greatest challenge.

Use this basic formula: tie in the lesson you're teaching to something with which the child is already familiar. Vary your tying-in technique to fit the subject and the age of the children.

Interest in reading can be created without the actual teaching of a lesson by making attractive books easily available.

Choral speaking is an excellent way to arouse the interest of a class in oral communication. Whenever the child gets all wrapped up in something and forgets about himself his self-consciousness is lessened and his timidity along with it.

Creating interest in written communication begins in the lower grades with little stories about objects with which the child is familiar.

Modern math is of itself interesting to children.

To create interest in basic, needed drill in arithmetic it may be necessary to use an entirely different technique—arouse *the child's fighting spirit!*

Chapter Five

Teaching Children
How to Do Research

Research is an impressive, heavy word. It evokes pictures of the scholar in his study, the scientist in his laboratory. The dictionary definition doesn't make it sound much better—". . . . a studious inquiry, having for its aim the discovery of new facts *and their correct interpretation.*" But in simple classroom language it means the way in which a child finds the answer to a question—how he looks up the information he wants. It's important that he know how to do this. I have seen hundreds of children get the "Let's look it up" habit in school and make it their regular method of operation.

CLASS RESEARCH BEGINS EARLY

Class research is taught in a simple form even in the kindergarten. Any topic in which the children display interest should be used. Questions and answers, pictures, stories, films—all simple, effective tools, are brought into play.

A BIRD AND A PIECE OF STRING

Miss Rourke's first graders have just returned from a walk around their school block and are discussing with the teacher some of the more interesting sights.

"I saw apples in a box outside a store," says Janie.

"There was a lady sweeping her sidewalk," says Peter.

"But best of all was a bird!" exclaims Ted. "It was pulling and pulling on a piece of string. And the string was around a bundle of newspapers!"

"Why did you like the bird best?" asks the teacher.

"Because it looked so funny," answers Ted, "and I wondered why the bird wanted the string."

"Maybe it was hungry," suggests one child. "Did it want to play with the string?" asks another. The majority of the class doesn't think much of these suggestions.

"I know, Miss Rourke," says quiet little Mary who seldom joins in any conversation. "I know because my mother and I have been watching a bird in our tree." (Rather a long statement from a first grader, but little Mary is different in many ways.) "The bird wants that string because it's building a nest."

"Would you like to tell us more about your bird, Mary?" asks Miss Rourke.

But Mary's usual shyness takes over again and she shakes her head. The others continue with the string idea:

"Does it really put the string in its nest?"

"How can a bird tie a string?"

"I thought a bird would use grass for its nest."

"I saw a nest with hard mud in it."

Then the teacher asks, "Do all birds build the same kind of nest?"

This is a puzzler, but Eric says that big birds build big nests and little birds build little nests. His classmates agree.

Miss Rourke goes to the library shelf and finds the bird book with its large, colorful pictures. There is a story about each of the birds and it shows them either on the nest or near it. Sometimes the eggs or the young are shown too. After the hubbub of excitement dies down Miss Rourke reads a story about the robin, for all her little ones have become familiar with this stout fellow. Now they will hear about its nest-building, its eggs ("robin's egg blue") and the food it finds for the babies. First grade research has begun in earnest. There will be more stories about birds and their nests, more pictures studied and discussed.

MISS ROURKE FOLLOWS UP THIS NEW INTEREST

1. The next day Miss Rourke took her first graders to the science room where there are three nests on exhibit, one of which is a little swinging basket, an oriole's nest, attached

to a small tree branch. Here is a new bird to be investigated, a new type of nest, a new song.

2. She arranged with the teacher in charge of visual aids to borrow a beautifully colored filmstrip that shows the robin, the oriole, and several other birds. The children saw close-ups of nests in trees and of how the hungry young are fed.

3. Some of the children brought their own bird books from home and had the pleasure of showing the pictures to their classmates.

4. Mary's mother invited the class to come and see the robin's nest in Mary's tree.

5. The music teacher lent the class her record of bird calls, and these first graders learned to recognize the songs of the robin and the oriole.

6. After a week of this type of research Miss Rourke and the children decided to prepare a scrapbook of pictures and two or three stories of their experiences which they dictated to the teacher.

7. With their teacher's help they prepared their own little table of contents for the scrapbook.

8. The finished product was put on display on their own library table and proudly presented to visitors.

9. A highlight of the project was the visit to the kindergarten when the first graders displayed their scrapbook to the smaller children and told them stories about birds.

This is the start of a pattern that will continue throughout their school career, and beyond:

1. an interesting topic
2. followed by research
3. culminating in a report to others

Although the word "research" has not actually been mentioned to the children this is exactly what they have embarked upon and they accept it as naturally as they would a new song or poem.

THAT FIRST VISIT TO THE LIBRARY

Research is a matter of using the library, and it is very important that children become familiar with this place and feel at home in it.

When first grade children start to use a reader their teacher plans a visit to the school library.

"Does anyone know where we will find the library room?" she asks.

"My sister says it's way upstairs," says Julie.

"What will we do in the library?" she asks.

"Look at books,"—"Look at pictures,"—"Be quiet." (This last remark is from Julie whose big sister keeps her well informed.)

"What do you think we will see in the library?"

"Lots of books,"—"Pictures,"—"Maybe tables,"—"Chairs."

So the first grade journeys to the school library. There the teacher leads her class from section to section.

"Here are the books for older children to read," she says. "Are they like our books?"

"No!"—"Ours are thinner,"—"Ours have big letters,"—"And big pictures!"

"And over here," says the teacher in an impressive whisper, "is your special corner. These are the books that we will read when we visit the school library. See the cute little cat on the cover of this book—look at the clown on this one—and here is a funny little hen!"

The teacher seats her children in the small chairs provided for them and reads a story of a puppy who thought he knew more than his wise mother.

On the next visit to the library these first graders will choose a book to take to the little low tables where they can turn pages and possibly find some surprise to show to the teacher and class. During each visit they will learn more about "library manners," and will find more books and pictures than they had thought existed. *They're getting the library background for research to come.*

USING THE TABLE OF CONTENTS

One of the first tools of research taught to little children is the table of contents. Of course it is a very simple table and they become familiar with it by means of drill. Soon they are able to find a certain story on a certain page. Make a game of teaching the table of contents:

"Put your finger on the story, 'Jack Goes to the Farm'—good, Joey. That's it, Alice."

"Does any boy or girl know a quick way to find which page to turn to so we can read the story?"

Several children know the answer to that one, so they have the opportunity to be "it" and ask their classmates where to find other stories listed on the page. After a few moments of this drill game the teacher shifts their attention to the actual finding of a story on the given page, and the game continues. How grown up a child feels when he picks up another book and discovers that it too has a table of contents!

MAKING THEIR OWN TABLE OF CONTENTS

As we read earlier in this chapter first year children can make their own table of contents when they prepare a class scrapbook. When Miss Rourke's class had prepared a simple table of contents for their scrapbook on birds, this important tool of research became an accepted fact—something that they would always expect to find in any book, something to be *used*.

USING THE INDEX

The use of the index is taught in first grade. The word "Index" does not appear in the little books, but in the back of the reader there is a page on which new words are listed with the number of the page on which each word first appears. You can use your drill game for six-year-olds and they soon learn to use the page to help them find what they want.

Preparing an index for their own little scrapbook might be too difficult for such young children. It's more complicated than making a table of contents, but they should learn the use of it.

SOME CHILDREN HAVE NEVER LEARNED TO USE THESE TOOLS

I have found children in the third and fourth grades who are unfamiliar with the use of a table of contents and an index. I stop all research and teach these skills until they know what the pages are for and how to use them. They pick up the skills quickly and are quite pleased with themselves when they no longer have to look all through a book but can locate any part of it with ease. A teacher should not assume that the class knows all about using something so elementary. If you find children in higher grades are not using the index in their various school books, don't wait! Start immediately to train them no matter what the grade may be.

Try this with your class:

1. Select a story of some length from their basic reader.

2. Have the children pretend that this story is a small book.

3. Prepare a table of contents treating the parts of the story as chapters in your "book."

4. Prepare an index in which names of people, places, events, etc. are listed alphabetically with the pages where they may be found.

5. Keep it simple. Have one committee take people; another, places; a third, the names of animals, birds, and plants that appear in the story.

6. The chairmen of the committees will have the job of assembling the data in alphabetical order.

Once they have done this they will automatically use an index. The lesson has been driven home.

THESE TOOLS ARE INVALUABLE FOR RESEARCH

Children do an ever-increasing amount of research as they reach higher grades and this skill is a *must*. Take Jonathan, for example. As part of his group's project on the expansion of the early United States he had been assigned the explorations of Lewis and Clark— a real plum! When I met with the group to discuss likely sources of information I suggested that Jonathan might use certain books, one of which contained material of special interest to him.

A day or two later he came to me and said, "The book you told me about has *nothing* about Lewis and Clark and I've been *all through it!*"

I took the book. "Let's have a look at the index." He and I found 16 references to Lewis and Clark in that one index!

When Jonathan reported on Lewis and Clark I asked him to make a booklet of his pictures and report. It was his own idea to prepare a simple index at the back of the booklet. He said to me, "You're not going to catch me on *that* again!"

Even if a class seems to be familiar with using the index pages occasional drill is still a good idea. Whenever a new book is distributed or some new additions to the class library appear check the ability of your class to use these two important sections of a book, the table of contents and the index.

USING THE DICTIONARY

A little preschool child can enjoy a picture dictionary. If you read it with him frequently he begins to associate a letter and a picture and takes great pride in telling one and all that "B" is a big round ball. One experienced first grade teacher warns that the "A is for apple" picture dictionary may lead to some confusion when the child tackles phonics in school.

"A is not for apple," she maintains. "A is for apron or ape."

She has a point there. At any rate, when the child is learning phonics the picture dictionary in his classroom will give him several sounds of "A" and pictures to illustrate each. The more advanced picture dictionary for second grade may include a short sentence or two in connection with the picture and accompanying sound. As the child becomes familiar with these simple dictionaries he comes to know the arrangements of letters in order. In other words he becomes aware of the alphabet, which is something he must know before the dictionary can become a useful tool.

The Junior Dictionary comes into use in the third or fourth grade. These books vary. Some are much more detailed than others. For example, one may have 20,000 words and another 40,000; one may show pictures without any way of comparing size of the objects and another may tell you that this is 1/10 of normal size (a good subject for a math lesson). Study with your class whatever dictionary you have fallen heir to. Drill with them, and the dictionary will be used more and more for reference and research.

You may find that the Junior Dictionary does not have some of the more unusual words that you and the children want to look up, perhaps in connection with science or current events. Have a College Dictionary on your desk for such emergencies and encourage them to use it. You'll soon find it necessary to put an extra copy in the classroom library. If an individual child has trouble using such a comprehensive edition perhaps he is not yet ready for it, but let him try if he wants to. You can always suggest that he ask Anne, or Mike, or Lou to help him find something.

Familiarize yourself in advance with whatever dictionary your class will use. Be sure *you* know how to use the pronunciation key before you start to give that type of drill. Are you sure *you* know how syllable division is indicated? In the College Dictionary there are such letters of explanation after a word as L, ME, GR. If a more inquisitive child asks you what they mean be sure you can tell him. It could lead him into fields of research he never knew existed.

THE MULTIMEDIA APPROACH TO LEARNING

Effective teachers have always combined many kinds of material for the children in their classes. They have always encouraged children to *look,* to question, to handle an interesting object. Effective teachers have always encouraged experiment whether it might be in plant life or in the use of a new word or idea. Perhaps the word "multimedia" was not always used, but its meaning is plain. A *medium* is something through which or by which something else is accomplished, or conveyed, or carried on, and the good teacher uses all available media.

As the child becomes more skilled in the simpler types of research we have been investigating his teacher encourages him to seek wider sources of information. Some of these are in the classroom library or in the school library. For other sources he may travel to places in his town or city with the class or with his parents —such places as museums, galleries, city government buildings, historic landmarks, public libraries.

USING ENCYCLOPEDIA

In your classroom you may have a set of encyclopedia. More likely you share a set with others on the grade. If this is so, let's hope it's cradled on a movable table so it can be wheeled easily from room to room. Even if the using of your set presents complications use it.

Never assume that the children know how to use this new tool. If a child has a set of encyclopedia at home it may be arranged alphabetically, while the school set may be arranged topically. Plan a lesson in the use of the books when they are first presented to the class. Let the children handle the books to get the feel of them. It might be well to remind the class of their earlier lessons on the care and handling of printed material. I would tell them how much the set costs; it commands additional respect.

1. Two children can sit together and share a book for this introductory lesson. (If you think it wise, even three might work together and then you will have enough books of one set to go around.)

2. List on the board three topics to be checked in each volume. See that each little group finds and takes notes on the material found.

3. Have the groups exchange volumes for further drill.

4. On your next visit to the school library repeat the lesson using a different set of encyclopedia.

As your class becomes more at ease in the use of this new research tool teach them how to use cross references. They will be fascinated with the discovery that one topic leads to another and to still another. Sometimes there seems to be no end to a simple topic. Also it seems that there is no such thing as a simple topic, as Miss DeWitt's fifth graders discovered.

A FIFTH GRADE COMMITTEE PREPARES A REPORT ON MAPS

Miss DeWitt's fifth graders have been reading of the voyages of the early explorers of the New World. The children find the illustrations of maps in use at that period amusing and the teacher tells them why the maps are so inaccurate. She explains that little of the New World had been explored, and she ties this in with the subject that will occupy so much of their time and thought in fifth grade—the development of the nation from a cluster of settlements to its expansion to the Pacific. She emphasizes the critical role maps played in this tremendous achievement.

Experience has shown Miss DeWitt that it's not practical to have many children hunting at one time in a classroom set of encyclopedia. She uses committees on such a project with excellent results. Four or five have easier access to the information and can report to the class on their findings.

There are several volunteers eager for the job, all boys. Miss DeWitt selects three but says the committee needs a girl to serve too. After some hesitation Janie says she will help if she can choose another girl to work with her. So now there are five. They meet with the teacher who explains the problem, and they list books which they think may have the information:

Our classroom encyclopedia
The atlas
Our social studies book
Stories of famous explorers
The dictionary
The globe

Each child is given a temporary assignment to start the ball rolling. Janie and Nancy head for the encyclopedia shelf, for the boys have gallantly agreed to give them first chance at the books. They open to "MAPS" and what do they see?

> **Maps—1.** Ancient—*Egyptian—Greek* (see *Ptolemy)—Iraq*
> **2.** European map makers—*Columbus—Prince John*
> *—Vespucci—Mercator*
> **3.** American map makers—*John Smith—Lewis Evans*
> *—John Mitchell*

As Janie and Nancy glance ahead and see the parade of names— Pike, Jed Smith, Lewis and Clark, Fremont, and on and on, they panic and head for their teacher for advice on how to use so many names.

Miss DeWitt had expected something of the sort. She calls the committee together for a consultation.

"The girls have been looking up the subject of maps," she announces, "and have found more than they expected. Each of the topics under the heading "MAPS" has a list of cross references under it. Let's put our heads together and see if we can figure out the best way to tackle the problem." ("Cross references" is a brand new term and the children will enjoy using it.)

With the teacher's guidance the immediate problem is solved. The girls take "European map makers" and are soon engaged in finding the reasons for making flat maps when the world is round. Somehow they will have to explain why a Mercator projection makes some bodies of land and water so much bigger than they have any right to be. (I have had children take the skin carefully from a grapefruit, a thick-skinned one, to illustrate what happens when it is flattened out. They understand when they see a round object flattened that top and bottom split, and that is the reason for the surprising size of, for example, Greenland.)

The boys are more interested in Indian fighters' maps, road maps, contour maps, and aerial maps. They choose topics and start research. The entire committee has learned a new term (cross references) to spring on their classmates. The chairman, Frank, will have the honor of explaining the use of cross references to the rest of the class during report time.

MAPS, CHARTS, AND GRAPHS

Some children of eight or ten like to help the family plan a trip in the car, and enjoy checking the road map as Dad drives. A child who enjoys reading maps learns a great deal from the experience of seeing real life roads unfold as the family car covers the miles.

When it comes to graphs and charts I have found that children of the fifth and sixth grades think they're fascinating. They enjoy reading the bars or lines of the graphs that hold so much information for the child who knows how to interpret them.

A SIXTH GRADE CLASS DOES LIVE RESEARCH WITH A PURPOSE

It has been the custom in one school to announce at the weekly assemblies the attendance average of each school in the district. This means something to the fifth and sixth graders but is of little interest to the third and fourth graders. The school's standing is not good as far as attendance is concerned, and Mr. Clark's sixth grade is discussing what could be done to improve it.

Carol says that her little brother in third grade stays home whenever he feels like it. If he thinks he may be late he carries on so that their mother lets him stay home.

Bert says you haven't seen anything unless you've seen his sister put on her "sick act" as he calls it. She's only seven, but if there's something on TV she wants to watch she can make her mother think she's really sick until it's too late to go to school.

Debbie complains that her neighbor's children stay home to go shopping, or to the dentist.

Mr. Clark agrees those things are so. "Some children definitely do stay home too easily," he says, "but, on the other hand we wouldn't want a sick child to come to school. You say you'd like to improve the school's attendance record. Where can we start?"

"We can go to the classrooms and talk to the children," suggests Joan.

"How about a prize for the highest average?" asks Dick.

"I have an idea," says Dennis. "Let's make a graph showing the average of each class every week!"

This appeals to the others. They have been making line and bar graphs in math and social studies. There is a graph on the bulletin board showing temperatures since September. Why not one for the school attendance averages? Mr. Harris, the principal, has announced in the assembly that the school has the lowest attendance average in the district.

"A graph used with a purpose is a good idea," says Mr. Clark. "You've studied graphs, you've made graphs—now let's put our experience to work. Let's make a list of the facts we must gather before we can make a graph that means something."

    1. How many classes will be shown on the graph?
    2. How many weeks will our campaign run?
    3. We'll need two graphs, one to show the poor attendance before the campaign and one to show the improvement, we hope.
    4. Which will show more clearly, a bar or a line graph?
    5. We must get the principal's permission to visit each class and explain the plan.

PLANNING THE BETTER ATTENDANCE CAMPAIGN

First things first. The class officers talked with Mr. Harris, the principal, who not only approved the project but promised them his support and free publicity. Then Janet and Ted visited the classrooms of all third to sixth grades. (It was decided that the smallest children would not be included this time. Possibly the good example of their older brothers and sisters would have more effect than a graph.)

A large bar graph was put in place near the assembly hall doors. It showed all too plainly the poor record of attendance from January 3 to the end of February. Over it was a sign reading "WE CAN DO BETTER!" Beside it the principal taped an office memo giving the averages of all the schools in the district. Yes, their school was the lowest.

Mr. Clark's class decided to prepare a weekly bar graph for March and April to be displayed at the other side of the assembly hall doors. There would be a new one each week showing the pre-

WE CAN DO BETTER!

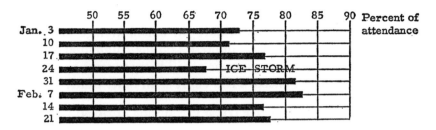

vious week's record. On it would be listed each class that took part in the campaign and just where it stood in comparison with the other contestants. Mr. Harris assured them that he would announce the weekly results at the assemblies, *and* he would suggest to each teacher that he or she make it a point to take the class to visit the graph frequently to check their relative position and to answer questions about the workings of percentages and bar graphs.

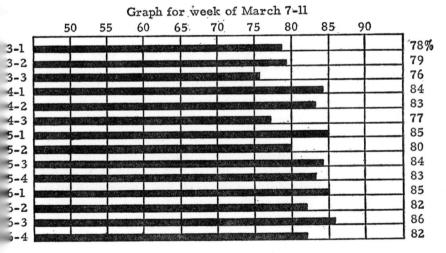

Average Attendance for Week 81.71%

The mystery of the black bars was explained to the younger children involved in the campaign and they became very much aware of how their own class stood in the weekly race. If an epidemic of sniffles kept 3–3 behind one week they were more anxious than ever to make good the following week. You can guess which sixth grade planned the project, but they too might fall behind because of a bit of bad luck.

Mr. Harris, eager as he is to have the school average in attendance climb out of last place, impresses on the children at assemblies that he does not want any who are ill to try to come to school. He does want them to make a real effort at all other times.

WHAT THE SIXTH GRADE LEARNED FROM THEIR CAMPAIGN

Here is an example of down to earth, practical research. A problem was presented—call it a challenge if you wish—and the class had to plan what to do first. They talked with the leaders involved, secured permission where necessary, searched out facts, decided what kind of campaign was needed, studied the most effective kind of display, and prepared and exhibited that display. Let's hope they get their reward—the pride that the entire school will feel in a successful undertaking.

COPYING FROM THE TEXT IS NOT RESEARCH

You'll have to be careful that children don't copy material word for word when they're doing research. When they find what they want in reference books there is a tendency to copy the whole business either painfully and slowly or in such an illegible scribble it means little to anyone. Get children to disdain such a time-wasting, boring, ineffective method of operation.

The time to teach the proper use of reference books is when the children first begin to use them. Such a simple method as, "Now close the book and tell me about it" should be started no later than the second grade. Here again we may make a game of it and still impress on little children the need for interpreting information in their own words. If they don't understand it, copying from the book will not help to clarify the meaning.

WHAT YOU CAN DO ABOUT THE PROBLEM

You say, "All right, but here I am stuck with a fifth grade that has no idea of the way to get information from a book and pass it on to others." And if I tell you to start using the method they never learned in second grade, or third, or fourth, you may answer, "But I'm right in the middle of research on Exploration. How can I possibly stop and teach them how to take notes?"

When *will* you do it? *When* will they learn the valuable lesson? Sixth grade? Or would junior high be the time?

Let's start now!

> ✔ Have a frank talk with your fifth graders. It's a delightful age, they'll love you for treating them like adults. Tell them they're on the wrong track and you know a better, shorter, *smarter* way to do it.

> ✔ Pick a topic; Henry Hudson will do. What do we need to know? For whom he sailed, when he sailed, what he found, when he found it, what were the results, why are the Hudson River and Hudson Bay both named after him when they are so far apart?

> ✔ How can you remember what you have read? Here's the secret. *Always do your research with a pencil in your hand.* Unfortunately, you can't write in the book, but you can and must write in your notebook. Put down a date as you read, a country, the names of people in the story. With a few notes in your hand and a bit of rehearsing alone before report time, you can get up and give an interesting account of Henry Hudson to the other children in the class.

> ✔ Study the wall map before you report so you can point out the explorations of this man.

Take these four steps in preparing the report and you will be ready for any reasonable question you may be asked about the subject because you have been over the principal ground.

You'll feel awfully good about the whole thing, just as you always do when you're well prepared.

One lesson with the class may be enough, depending on your class. You will know from the results whether or not they need more coaching. The more able readers will get the idea and can pass along the new approach to those who take a little longer to catch on. If one of your good readers offers to help someone find material give him your blessing.

THE SKILL OF SKIMMING—A VITAL AID TO RESEARCH

Skimming is a skill and should be taught under your guidance just as any skill has to be taught. There is a danger that a fast reader may be a careless reader but if he is *trained* to read fast he will not be careless and will be able to cover a maximum amount of material with a minimum of wasted time and effort.

Try your group of top readers on this—*they deserve attention too.*

> 1. Select a topic of interest. For your first lesson with them let all take the same topic. When they are more familiar with this technique each may choose his own topic.
> 2. Give the group a few minutes to find the books they need for their research.
> 3. What are we looking for? Jot down in your notebooks several questions you want answered.
> 4. Now read quickly with these questions in mind. Pause only when your eye catches a word or phrase that signals something you're looking for.
> 5. Read the word or phrase again to see if it is what you want. If it is, jot it down in your notebook.
> 6. Continue reading as fast as you can, pausing only when you find another piece of information you want to jot down.

Your good readers will enjoy this technique. You will find that they use more and more books in their research and have more information to contribute. If they show any desire to help a child who is struggling along trying to prepare a report, encourage them to lend a hand. Just keep an eye on the situation to make sure the slower reader doesn't let his helper do all the work.

"PENCIL IN HAND" READING

Anyone who reads intelligently and effectively likes to mark certain passages in his book. A smart gentleman of our acquaintance buys second-hand books for several reasons—they're cheap, he feels better about marking them up, and he enjoys looking for the underlining and paragraph scoring done by a previous reader. There are countless others who maintain that reading a book without marking statements that impress you is a waste of time.

In our public school systems books are a large part of the budget, and Heaven help the child who defaces one! In front of each volume a child receives there is a paster with names, classes, and dates of the procession of children who have already used it, plus "Condition when received" and "Condition when returned."

I am not recommending that children be permitted to deface books, but what a blessing it would be if they were able in some way to make them their own. To show how ridiculous the situa- tion can get, take the workbook. We call it a workbook, but don't write in it because it's new and it has to last a long time. Fold a paper and write your answers on the paper next to the question in the workbook . . . Can you top that?

I recall the time we were cleaning out a stock room and I found a set of workbooks suitable for use in my grade. They had seen some use but had not been written in. I presented them to my class telling them, "They're yours to use and keep. And you may write in them." The children were surprised and overjoyed. A workbook to write in and to keep!

There are parents who feel so strongly about this situation that they buy a set of books that the child can use at home and mark up as he sees fit, underlining parts of sentences and checking para- graphs that will help him put together the data he wants. But in most cases we don't have workbooks to write in. Train your chil- dren to have a notebook handy when doing research, whether it's a visit to a museum, a conversation with an authority on a given subject, or reading for information.

COMBINING THE ACCUMULATED DATA

Now it's time to prepare the report. The child brings into play the knowledge he's gained from research and the skills he's ac- quired in composition, both oral and written.

Let's look into the problems Robert met and solved when he prepared a report on clothing in cold countries to present to his class:

    1. With notebook and pencil in hand he checked the en- cyclopedia for such topics as Alaska, Yukon, seal, walrus, polar bear, to find out all he could about his "clothing problem."

    2. He read a book about an Eskimo boy, taking notes as he read.

    3. He hunted through tables of contents and indexes in social studies books jotting down topics and pages as he proceeded.

    4. He talked with his father's friend who had spent his Army career in Alaska.

5. He visited the local furrier for a possible scrap of seal-skin
6. He spent an afternoon at the museum with his family.

Robert reported to his class on the subject of clothing worn in cold countries. He pointed out on the wall map the cold countries he was about to discuss. He told how Eskimos hunt for the furs needed for warmth and proudly displayed two scraps of sealskin, one natural and one dyed. Then Robert's friend, Fred, helped him show a set of pictures borrowed from the local library illustrating the use of furs by people who live in cold countries. Robert explained the details of the pictures and answered questions.

For his next book report the boy plans to write about the story of the Eskimo child, the same book he used to help him with the research on clothing.

A child with a "hot country" ethnic background might prefer research on animals, clothing, food, or shelter in such a land. The basic plan would vary only slightly.

ABILITY TO USE DATA IMPROVES TOO

As children advance in grade and in the skills of research we can expect more elaborate use of the data they accumulate when hunting for information. In junior high and later, a young person who has been trained properly in such skills may pursue a topic at great length in the library, museum, or the laboratory. It may even lead some of them to find their life work.

—— SOME HIGHLIGHTS TO REMEMBER ——
ABOUT RESEARCH

Research in the elementary grades is the way in which a child finds the answer to a question.

As soon as children learn to read they should be helped to acquire the "Let's look it up" habit.

The school and classroom libraries are sources of information. Even in first grade the teacher makes her children feel at home there and helps them to love books.

In order to make the most effective use of books, children should be taught from the earliest grades to refer to the table of contents and the index.

Dictionaries and encyclopedias are important tools of research, but children must be taught how to use them.

Graphs, charts, and maps can explain a situation to the child who knows how to read them.

Many media are used in class research—textbooks and storybooks, dictionaries, encyclopedias, pictures, films, visits to places of interest, and the simple question and answer.

Children must be taught to take notes when they read. If they copy from the text the habit can be corrected by proper training.

"Skimming" the text is a vital aid to improved research. This is a skill and has to be taught to children.

Encourage "pencil in hand," not only in reading, but in any type of research.

Chapter Six

Using Audio-Visual Aids

eachers are always on the lookout for material that will make their teaching more meaningful. They look for something with an appeal to the eye or an appeal to the ear—something that will catch a child's attention—something that will capitalize on those two ready channels, the eye and the ear, to help put the lesson across.

Years ago a good teacher made his own material when nothing else was available and when possible took his classes to see firsthand the subject of the lesson. Henry Thoreau, for example, took his pupils on nature walks. Accounts written years later by his former students show the effectiveness of the method.

Modern teachers have aids at their disposal that were scarcely thought of a generation ago. Some are improvements of old aids to teaching, many are new, and all are effective *if the teacher knows how, and where, and when to use each one.* They range from maps to television, from travel posters to tape recordings, from puppets to field trips. Used intelligently they are valuable aids to teaching. Used without planning or purpose they are little more than time-wasting entertainment!

LEARN HOW TO USE THE MACHINES

In order to do a good job here you *must* be familiar with the most effective aids available, know where to find them and how to use them. If an in-service course in the use of audio-visual aids is available it is the best way to learn how to handle the various types of machines. One can learn from experience too, but it's a long process, and it's difficult to hold interest and keep order when you're fumbling with tapes and looking for the right buttons.

Let's examine some of the audio-visual aids to teaching. There are so many kinds that one could never find out *all* there is to know about *all* of them, but we can consider those that the classroom teacher is most likely to be using and discuss the advantages and disadvantages of each.

USING THE "STILL" PICTURE

This old reliable is invaluable! A young teacher may turn up her nose at the suggestion that she use so old-fashioned an aid to a lesson—but wait a minute. There are many types of still pictures and more than one way of showing them to your class.

PHOTOGRAPHS

1. The still picture has been called "a frozen slice of life." It is there to be used when it is impossible to experience the situation firsthand. Pictures, carefully chosen, will help you launch a new unit of work—the type of unit that the curriculum may require but which has to be artificially introduced. Some units of work come naturally as a center of interest. Others, such as Eskimo life, or the Amazon Valley, may need an outside stimulus to get them started, and here your still picture serves well.

2. When a child is doing research, pictures help him to understand his subject. If he is a less than average reader the pictures in the book explain much that he may miss in the text. And when he reports to the class on his research (good reader or poor) pictures chosen with your assistance will help create interest in the topic, and will explain to the class points that the child making the report might not clarify. A good picture is "worth a thousand words."

3. Be sure that the picture gives a true impression of what you are trying to put across. Do the Dutch usually wear wooden shoes, or is this a holiday type of dress shown in the picture? Is all Brazil a vast, impenetrable jungle? Is there anything in the picture you have selected that will give a child a true idea of the size of a polar bear? Choose your own illustrations carefully and help the children choose theirs.

LIBRARY FILES OF STILL PICTURES

Your school library probably has a file of mounted pictures available. If you have been appointed recently or have transferred from a different school it would be a good idea to talk with the teacher in charge of the library. Find out whether or not there is a file of pictures mounted and waiting to be used.

In one school that had been open at least five years there had never been enough time to work on such a project. The teacher in charge of the library had so many other jobs, and a class, that she despaired of ever finding the time. During a conference with the president of the Parents' Association whose child was in her class she happened to mention the problem. Within a week a group of five volunteer mothers appeared and offered their help. The school now has a fine file of pictures, all mounted, and available to any class that needs them.

Check with the town library also. It is almost certain to have a file of mounted pictures from which the children may borrow what they need. Some librarians require a note from the teacher before a child is permitted to borrow a set of pictures, but that's a small price to pay.

Suppose you want to show still pictures to your class. For example, you have a colorful illustration of Chief Powhatan and Captain John Smith doing a bit of trading. How much more it means if you project a magnified picture so your whole class can study it at the same time, and can discuss the situation and ask and answer questions.

THE OPAQUE PROJECTOR

This machine projects nearly anything up to 6″ by 6″ in size. A colored picture, black and white, a page from a book, specimens of handwriting, leaves, charts, maps—the list is long. A drawing or painting (but not larger than 6″ by 6″) can be projected while you or the children trace the outline and make that large map or drawing you have been needing.

Why isn't the opaque projector used more often? Good question! It is heavy to cart around from room to room. A very dark room is necessary for a good projection. You are limited in the size of the picture you can use. Unless you use it properly the object being projected may curl up in the intense heat from the bulb.

Despite these shortcomings the advantages are so great that it's worth spending some time learning how to use the machine properly.

THE OVERHEAD PROJECTOR

Many schools order the overhead projector to replace their old, faithful opaque machine when it finally wears out. There is a distinct advantage here as the teacher may sit at his desk *with* the projector, face his class, and point out *on the copy in the machine* whatever he wishes to bring to the attention of his pupils. It has all the advantages of the opaque projector and eliminates some of the "bugs."

FIILMSTRIP PROJECTOR

Here's a machine that's a blessing, pure and simple! It's light in weight, easy to operate, can be shown in the average classroom equipped with window shades, and often comes with an extra gadget that can be attached for showing 2″ by 2″ slides. There is a wealth of filmstrips from which you may choose or make your own slides. (More about that a little later.)

The filmstrip can be shown to kindergarteners or sixth graders. You can operate it easily yourself while you carry on the lesson. If you prefer, one of your dependable students can take charge of the machine while you give your full attention to the class.

IDEAS FOR USING FILMSTRIPS

1. To introduce a subject: When presenting the study of linear measures the filmstrip graphically dramatizes the romantic history: the "foot" measure as of an average Roman soldier, the "yard" measure from the tip of an English king's nose to the end of his arm, and so on.

2. To enrich a study: Miss Rourke (Ch. 5) used a colored filmstrip to show her little first graders close-ups of the birds and nests they were studying and how the young were fed.

3. As the culmination of a study (or a review): To tie up any loose ends of a unit on ways of travel the filmstrip takes the children along in a dugout canoe on a jungle river or a dogsled in the Arctic; from an Indian travois to a transcontinental bus; from stagecoach to a jet liner.

MORE ADVANTAGES OF THE FILMSTRIP

✔ The pictures in the tiny roll can be projected for as long a time as you need to explain them and answer or ask questions.

✔ You can turn back to any picture you wish simply with a flick of the wrist.

✔ The list of available film strips is extensive and varied. Your school probably adds to its library of films as often as money is forthcoming.

Are there any disadvantages? I can think of one, but it's not the fault of the machine—it's human frailty. The last person who used the film may possibly have put it back in the container either upside down or backwards. It's annoying to you and amusing to your class—which doesn't help the lesson at all. Be sure to take a moment to check before you show the film—it's worth it.

THE 2″ BY 2″ SLIDE

The 2″ by 2″ slide deserves its popularity. There is an attachment that comes with most filmstrip machines that enables you to use such a slide easily.

Lists of 2″ by 2″ photographic slides are available from your teacher in charge of visual aids or from the school office. One great advantage of these slides is that you can arrange them in any sequence you desire, while in a filmstrip you must use the pictures as they appear or skip past any you don't want or need for your lesson.

Another advantage—your color slides can be shown without having to move one of the more cumbersome machines.

Children can make their own little slides to illustrate a report, a class excursion, or other activity. The slide can be made of etched or clear glass. The picture can be drawn in pencil and traced on the glass, then filled in with the desired shades of India ink. Sometimes children illustrate their own reports in this way and get a real thrill out of the project. The slide can be washed and is ready to be used again. If it's a good one keep it for another time.

If you want to go all out on the 2″ by 2″ slide have your color photographs of a Spring Festival or an athletic event prepared professionally and your school can "immortalize" the memorable event for its collection.

MICROPROJECTORS

Just a word or two about this machine which is usually an attachment placed on a microscope to project (and of course enlarge) an object that otherwise could be seen by only one child at a time. In this way the entire group can see the difference between the fibers of flax and wool, for example, or study the composition of a flower petal.

The microprojector is not as widely used in elementary schools as in junior high, but if your school has one you will find it worthwhile. Teachers of science say it is of great value to their students as any tiny object can be observed by all at the same time and can be studied under the teacher's guidance.

MOVING PICTURES AS AN AID TO TEACHING

Children see so many movies that one would think they'd be blasé about any film you might choose to show. Strangely enough this is not the case, for your class is very much interested in historical movies and documentaries too. It's all in the way you present the subject.

As in the case of the projected photograph or the filmstrip, the movie may be shown to *introduce* a subject, to *enrich* it, or as a *culmination* or *review,* but no matter when you plan to present it to your class you *must* preview the film. This not only eliminates the guesswork as to just what the movie will show, but it enables you to prepare your introduction and the discussion that is sure to follow the showing.

Suppose your class has been studying the events leading to the American Revolution. They've seen pictures in their social studies books and library books. They know something of colonial customs and dress. They know a bit about such patriots as Franklin, Jefferson, Washington, Patrick Henry. And now you have a film for them in which they will hear one of Henry's famous speeches.

Tell your class about the great treat in store for them. List on the board some of the objects the children think they may see in the picture:

Famous people	Colonial buildings
Soldiers	People on horseback
Beautiful dresses	People in coaches

List the questions they ask:

Will we see the king of England?
Will Patrick Henry really make a famous speech?
Will Washington be there?
Will there be a battle?

There is a sense of anticipation before a movie begins. The dark window shades are tightly drawn, the last skirt straightened, the last ankle scratched. There is the whir of the machine that everyone unconsciously awaits, and the picture flashes on the screen.

Here is a street in colonial Virginia—Richmond, in fact. A group of men in the fancy dress of the times discusses the latest indignities imposed by the English crown. Beautiful carriages pass in the background, drawn by shining horses and attended by Negro footmen in elaborate uniforms. Here and there a lady may be seen stepping carefully along the roughly cobbled street. ("Oh's" and "Ah's" from the girls as they notice the velvet and laces of her gown.)

A man in simple, brown clothes approaches on horseback, his mount tired and mud-spattered. His head is bent as though in deep thought. A stir is seen in the group of men.

"That's Patrick Henry."

"Wonder what he has up his sleeve today."

"Do you remember that speech he made about the Stamp Act?"

"He'll go too far one of these times. He'll find himself in England on trial for treason!"

Our scene shifts to St. John's Church, and the eye is given time to feast on the beautifully simple colonial interior. Another group of men stands talking, and it is clear that they do not agree with each other on the topics being discussed. Now and then the young movie audience catches the sound of a familiar name and heads nod in satisfaction.

The Virginia Convention is called to order and Mr. Henry asks to be recognized by the chairman. He comes forward, mounts the steps to the pulpit and begins to talk—quietly at first. The movie audience is motionless. Which speech will this be? All of them are exciting just to read about. The children remember when they dramatized—but now the voice is rising, the camera flashes from one face to another. Expressions of anger, doubt, joy, flash on the screen. Here it comes—

"Is life so dear, or peace so sweet, as to be purchased at the price of chains and slavery? Forbid it, Almighty God! I know not what course others may take, but as for me, give me liberty, or give me death!"

The film ends but the audience is strangely quiet. When the lights come on there is a tentative clapping of hands. Then the applause becomes unanimous.

"Do you want to talk about it?" asks the teacher.

Do they! Eddie is almost two years behind in reading, but his eyes are shining. Susie is a precocious know-it-all but she is dabbing at tears that she wants no one to see. Fred, the talkative, born salesman type, is silent and thoughtful.

Then the comments and questions start:

"I thought everyone in the colonies hated the king."

"Did Patrick Henry go to jail?"

"How soon after this did the Revolution begin?"

"I'd like to have a dress like that lady wore!"

"What a beautiful church!"

"Is it still there?"

Nothing but a movie could have caused such a reaction. What other medium could have picked up these children and put them down in a period of history to live the event with the people in the church. How could Eddie with his stumbling reading ever have hoped to understand the power of the words he has just heard? Who but Patrick Henry in person could have rendered Fred powerless to comment for a moment?

THE RIGHT MOVIE AT THE RIGHT TIME IS PRICELESS

1. Encourage your class to talk about the movie and let them ask and answer questions.

2. Check your lists on the board to see if the children have come close to guessing what would be in the film.

3. Have an art lesson soon—costumes, St. John's Church, a colonial street scene.

4. Try writing "You Are There" accounts of the event.

The story of Patrick Henry's brave speech shown to a group of children who have been doing research and reporting on the causes of the American Revolution will make a great impression on them. They will always remember the color and excitement of this moment of history.

DIFFICULTIES YOU MAY MEET

The person in charge of ordering films for your school does his best but he cannot work miracles. If your school is like most I know you request a film for an approximate date—perhaps months ahead, and hope you will get it when you need it. Then you go ahead and plan your work so that you will not be completely dependent upon any film. If it arrives before you are ready for it, or after your need is past history, you change your approach—do the best you can to make it worthwhile. *Great are the occasions when everything works out right.*

There are other difficulties that you should be prepared to meet. Have you taken the time to preview this film? Can you run the projector? Can you mend a broken film if necessary? Independence is wonderful!

KEEP A CARD FILE OF FILMS

If your school doesn't have a card file of films that have been shown, start your own, and ask the others on the grade to keep a file too. It's not involved. On 3″ by 5″ cards put down the name of the film, the grade using it, the date shown, and a brief comment on the content of the film. This will prove valuable to others and yourself next year or the year after. It would be a time-saver to jot down the source of the film, and then you won't have to look through catalogs to find out where to order it.

RADIO BROADCASTS FOR YOUR CLASS

For some of us the radio broadcast is a mixed blessing. If you are "lucky" enough to work in a more modern school that has a loudspeaker in every room and a control panel in the main office you just *may* get to hear some of the programs you want.

A number of large cities have a "School of the Air" and broadcast excellent programs to their schools. In the area around the cities other schools in smaller communities can pick up these broadcasts. Booklets, prepared at considerable expense, are provided for teachers which help you plan ahead and prepare your class to hear certain programs. There will be a story hour, a sing-along, a science period, observation of holidays, etc. There are different times for the several grade levels to listen. The programs are well thought out and beautifully prepared. What could possibly go wrong?

HOW TO RUIN A BROADCAST

When you plan your day with the class you list on the board the radio broadcasts you expect to hear. One day there may be two, another day there may be one or none. Then you take the time to talk about the coming program and prepare your class to appreciate it. You conscientiously set aside time for it. When the hour arrives notebooks are out and ready and you are standing at the board chalk in hand. What happens? Any of the following—maybe you can add to the list:

- The program comes over perfectly—you enjoy it and have an ideal follow-up.
- The boy in charge is absent or forgot to look at the time —result, no program.
- You wait, nothing happens, you nod to your monitor who is trained to go downstairs and find out what's wrong.
- The broadcast starts, it's too soft, then it blasts on, then off. By this time your class is getting pretty silly.
- It starts 12 minutes late.

None of this is the fault of the radio station, nor is it the fault of the people who work so hard to prepare fine educational programs for the schools. It certainly isn't the teacher's fault. But it happens frequently and it's a shame. But still and all the advantages are great. Plan time for the programs. Use the programs. Is television any luckier?

THE PROS AND CONS OF TELEVISED PROGRAMS

A great deal of money is spent to provide schools with good TV sets. Sometimes Parents' Associations present them to their schools.

Sometimes there is a fund raising campaign. How ideal it would be if each classroom had a set, but that day has not arrived.

Lessons are presented by experts in their field. There is art for the small fry, art for the middle grades. It suffers somewhat in black and white TV, but the teacher watching the program is able to gain helpful hints and some new ideas. The instructor who presents science lessons on TV chooses his material carefully with the age of his audience in mind. He has at his fingertips all the equipment needed for demonstrations—from live pets to live experiments. At the end of the lesson he usually leaves the children in the classes with a challenge to try out a certain experiment on their own.

French and Spanish lessons are presented for the various age levels and the instructors encourage the children in the TV audience to speak too. They may pretend that the pronunciation is not quite right and have the children repeat several times. One has the impression that the instructor is right there with you. Booklets are provided for the classroom teacher and ideally the lessons should become part of your planning each day.

Now let's look at the flaws, for it's better to be prepared for the worst if necessary. The flaws are not in the lessons as presented, but in their reception and carry-over:

TV programs don't wait for you—they begin whether you're there or not. You try to make it on time, but should you interrupt a child who's finishing a report that has caused him much sweat and tears? Can you stop a class in the middle of a test? Heaven knows you tried to time it right but the fire drill threw everything out of balance.

Today you leave in plenty of time to get your class settled (you're in a school with one TV set and that's in the auditorium). You find another class there practicing for an assembly program. By the time explanations and excuses are exchanged seven minutes of your lesson time have flown, and you and your class are watching the end of an experiment about which you know nothing.

Suppose there is a TV set right in your classroom. The French lesson starts at 11:30, and at 11:50 your lunchroom children must be on their way with the endless paraphernalia that seems to be part of their heritage. The lesson is wasted for those who go and those who remain with you.

And about the carry-over: with all good intentions you resolve that you will use the fine suggestions given you by the TV instructor. You'll try to find a spot in your overflowing program. In order to do it something else will have to go. What will it be? Try the suggestions in Chapter 3, "Planning Your Work," for the TV and radio programs are *good.* It would be a shame not to let your children have the benefit of them. And it would be too bad to omit either the discussions that precede a program or the follow-up suggested by the instructor.

I cite the shortcomings so you will know there may be setbacks and not become discouraged. Try to overcome such shortcomings— avoid them if possible. Despite them I use radio and TV programs to great advantage.

CLOSED CIRCUIT TV

Each year more school systems are able to put closed TV circuits into their schools. Special lessons in English are being presented to classes with foreign language problems. There are programs for the mothers of these children too.

Lessons in child care and meal planning are given to the older girls and their mothers in slum area schools.

Cost is the big difficulty, but there is a steady increase in the number of closed circuit units being installed and in the variety of ways in which they can be used to improve education.

TV AFTER SCHOOL HOURS

Space shots sometimes coincide with school hours and you would plan to have your class watch the blast-off and the exciting few minutes that follow. If such an event is coming up at a time when children are at home be sure to have them write the day and the time in their notebooks. Encourage them to bring in newspaper and magazine pictures and articles for their bulletin board.

Encourage a fifth or sixth grade class to listen to one newscast a day.

If there is a special children's play to be shown in early evening hours or on a weekend, plan ahead with your children so that they will want to watch it at home. Discuss the playwright or one of the actors. Give them a preview of what they may expect to see and hear. Assign a short, simple homework lesson—not enough to make them dislike the program, but definite enough to be important.

Perhaps a children's concert is to be presented on TV. Talk about the conductor. Take one of the selections listed and tell your class the story of it, or tell them to be prepared to describe the way their favorite instruments performed in the concert.

LEARN TO USE THAT TAPE RECORDER

The tape recorder is a machine of many uses—good uses. Almost anyone can operate the small, compact ones, but the larger models offer some slight complications to the beginner, and the older the model the more difficult it is to operate. If you are unfamiliar with tape recorders make it your business to learn how to handle them. They are a joy and a blessing.

Have you ever watched a child's face as he hears his voice on the tape? It's a study in pleasure and self-consciousness. He's a little embarrassed but he never wants you to shut it off.

IDEAS FOR CLASSROOM USE OF THE TAPE RECORDER

1. Class 3–2 has learned the delightful poem, "The King's Breakfast" by A. A. Milne and is working on a choral speaking arrangement of it. Their teacher, Miss Engel, makes a tape of their efforts and the children listen to it and criticize one or two parts—"Too loud," "Can't understand the words," "Our voices are too high." After three more recordings of the poem they are pleased. Will Miss Engel play it for their parents at the meeting next week?

2. Mr. Jansen, a young teacher with a knack for that sort of thing, volunteers to record certain "School of the Air" radio programs while his own class listens to them. These tapes are available to any teacher who may have missed the program or whose children want to use the material in their research. When too many tapes are collected the best are filed and the other tapes reused by recording another program over them. (The unwanted recording is easily erased by playing another program over the old one.)

3. The speech teacher who visits one day a week keeps a progress report of each child on tape. The children in her

speech improvement classes hear their own voices and their own errors. When there is an improvement in a speech defect the child can hear it immediately and is more encouraged than when he goes along from week to week not knowing how he's doing.

4. A teacher in charge of a fine glee club tapes some of the performances at assemblies and Spring Festivals. She uses the tape recorder at rehearsals and finds it a help to the children in correcting poor singing habits. It helps the instructor too, for she is able to hear on the tape errors that are not discernible while she is directing or playing the piano.

School districts have begun to compile tape libraries of music, literature, special events, etc. and are making a great number of worthwhile tapes available to the schools.

THE FIELD TRIP OR "EXCURSION" AS A TEACHING AID

Children love field trips. To those whose parents never take them anywhere it is a red letter occasion, and strangely enough those living in an overprivileged community are thrilled at the prospect of a trip to almost anywhere. First graders can get excited about an excursion to the school garden. Third graders never forget the experience of sliding down a real live fire pole with a fireman waiting below to catch them. Fifth and sixth graders hire buses or take the subway and visit museums, historical sites, City Hall. Some go to Washington, D.C. I read of a class that took a plane ride to study their community from the air.

CAN A TRIP BE EDUCATIONAL AND FUN TOO?

It's all up to you. Can you control your class *outside* of the building? I have met teachers on trips who screamed like banshees to keep a class in some semblance of order; and others who had their children marshalled in lockstep; and still others who walked along serenely while a happy group of children chatted, each with his own buddy for the day, notebook under arm, looking forward to the next sight the teacher had planned for them.

In all fairness, some classes are harder to manage than others. Know your group before you take on an assignment such as an all day trip with them. Try a visit to the local library first. Just keep your eyes open and your mouth shut, and you'll know soon enough who has a tendency to get out of hand when outside the walls of his school. It could be that you will have to leave him behind when you venture forth next time.

PREPARING FOR A FIELD TRIP

✔ *Never take your class anywhere unless you know you are expected.* Contact the people at the receiving end first to make sure you will be welcome and that a suitable time can be arranged. This holds true whether you plan to visit the boiler room, a museum, another classroom, or City Hall.

✔ *Don't* go just because another teacher is planning a trip and wants you to go along with your group for company.

✔ *Don't* go just to get out of the classroom for a day. If your class is hard to manage try to picture what they'll be like on the street or in the subway.

✔ *Do* plan to take a field trip when that is the best way to teach some definite topic and it can be seen, heard, or touched rather than reading about it or seeing pictures of it.

I recall seeing a group of children with their teacher in a supermarket in a run-down section of a large city. One little group seemed to have a list of groceries to buy. The treasurer, not a day over nine in age, clutched a small purse. As I came near to eavesdrop he was complaining that "Joey wants to buy something for the party that costs more than we allowed for." Joey defended his choice saying that it was a bigger bag. The teacher arbitrated the dispute so quietly that I was unable to hear, but the boys seemed to accept her decision and the shopping continued. Joey carried the basket containing crackers, cheese, powdered milk, paper cups, and gumdrops. I watched them at the check-out counter and out the door. How much more meaningful the little excursion was to this class than an unnecessary, expensive bus trip might be to another group.

✔ *Prepare your class for the trip.* Be sure they know why they are going and what they may expect to see and do. If you are visiting the museum, even if you know there will be a guide, discuss the subject of the trip with your children. Have them list in a small pocket size notebook some pertinent questions. The guide will appreciate the forethought and the children will gain a great deal more.

✔ *Settle possible behavior misunderstandings before you leave the building.* Have the class draw up a set of reasonable rules of conduct and encourage everyone to take part in the discussion. The children *must* know what is expected of them on the trip and *you must demand that of them.* If you are the kind of teacher who can discipline with a look you should have little trouble. Not all of us can do this, but never stoop to making an example of a child on a city street or in a cafeteria. *Know your children and your own ability to control them* before you venture away from the protective walls of the school building.

✔ *Settle the question of money with the class.* As you do when drawing up rules of conduct, have a serious class discussion about money. Your regular expenses—bus, admission, lunch, etc., make a perfect math lesson. But the question of how much they take along for extras must be settled by the group—and make them stick to it.

A sixth grade class of mine had agreed that 50 cents was plenty to spend for a souvenir of this particular trip. I noticed Wally spending money at the souvenir counter like a drunken sailor. When I questioned him he said carelessly that his father had given him $5 and told him to go ahead and have a good time. His classmates were indignant and brought him up on charges at the next class meeting. Too severe? No. He tried to put the blame on his father but the others wouldn't buy that. He knew the rules, and he would have to comply with them or not go on trips.

✔ *Get the necessary slips signed*—parental consent, superintendent's okay, whatever is required by your principal and well in advance of the date. A trip can be one of your most satisfying aids to effective teaching. John Dewey says, "An ounce of experience is worth a ton of theory." *

THERE ARE OTHER VISUAL AIDS, TOO

One handy visual aid right at our fingertips is so common that you may not think of it as such—the blackboard! In my own experience, when the blackboard is covered with ideas and not beautiful to behold we are doing our best thinking. When teacher and class are making initial plans for a unit of work where do we turn? Most likely we use our old reliable friend—the blackboard.

So many other aids, audio or visual, are around us all the time that we tend to forget them when we list the more spectacular

---

* Democracy and Education, MacMillan Company.

ones. But what about a good textbook? A globe? A wall map? Do you make use of those exhibt cases that are delivered to the schools by the museums? The charming little dioramas that show some phase of human, or animal, or plant life in three perfect dimensions? Have you tried making simple dioramas in the classroom? (See Chapter Seven.)

And what about puppets? Even small children love to make and maneuver the simpler hand puppets (See Page 120). Do puppeteers come to your school and delight all ages with their skill in telling the story of Treasure Island, or perhaps Tom Sawyer? Master Skylark? Punch and Judy? If not, make some inquiries at the school office and find out how to arrange this great treat.

TAKE ADVANTAGE OF THE HELP OF AUDIO-VISUAL AIDS

If you are newly appointed, or even if you have years of experience, learn all you can about the use of these aids to better teaching. Perhaps you have fumbled along with the various machines, depending on your busy teacher friends to help out in a crisis. It is a far from ideal arrangement.

Here is a golden opportunity to put that "promise to yourself" technique to work. Promise yourself *in writing* that this is the year you will take an in-service course in audio-visual aids, the course you have been putting off because it's given at a distant school or at an inconvenient time. You will be much more pleased with yourself, and you will be able to do so much more for your class. *Independence is wonderful!*

ELECTRONIC AIDS TO TEACHING

Everywhere we turn it seems that we read about the big changes that are in store for education through the increased use of electronic aids. Some wonder if teachers will be replaced as many workers in other fields have been. Others maintain that electronics can never replace the human touch so necessary in training children. Experts in the field say that a new day is dawning that can change the teacher from an overworked drudge into a counselor and advisor.

Let's have a look at some of the marvels already in the market. They are now being tested in schools to see if they can accomplish what is expected of them. Some have proved their worth. Possibilities seem endless.

THE TALKING TYPEWRITER

The talking typewriter derives its name from the fact that it has a touch-type keyboard (in seven colors). It also has a screen, speaker, and voice recorder.

A child's first experience with such a machine is an exploratory period with a teacher. Each feature is explained and tried. Then the talking typewriter is "locked."

Now a word appears on the screen, the word "TAKE." The voice says, "Take—T–A–K–E—take. Type the word take." If the child types it correctly the word appears on the screen or the voice tells him he is correct. If he makes an error the keys do not respond.

It can be programmed for reading, language, math, a foreign language. It can be used by children during school hours or in the evening by adults who want to improve their skills. The machine allows each individual to proceed at his own rate. It can be programmed to speak with the voice of a woman, a man, or a child, whichever is most suitable for the person using the machine.

Two big questions face the educators:

Is this to be used for drill or for the whole educational process?

Who will program these machines? Will it be in the hands of educators or will business do the programming?

COMPUTERS FOR DRILL

In experimenting with the use of computers for drill in math, for example, the machine is able to do what no human being ever could. It allows each child to proceed at his own rate because the computer quickly finds the individual's "track" and goes on from there. As soon as that "track" is successfully mastered the machine goes to the next level. It is endlessly patient and never tires.

It would be impossible for any teacher to find the daily level of drill needed for each student—but the computer can. The more able pupil need not waste time in unnecessary review. The less efficient neither holds back his classmates nor feels embarrassment at his lack of comprehension. It is a private affair.

Teachers question the ultimate value of the "drill machine" as some call it. "Who will keep after the child who dreams and never does anything without nagging?" "Isn't it a very lonely way for a child to learn?" "After the novelty wears off won't the child miss the competition of his classmates or the physical presence of a teacher?"

No one knows the answers to all the questions. A great deal of experimentation has to be done and much data assembled.

COMPUTERS FOR MARKING

Computerized tests are marked by computers, but at the present time the teacher still has to record such marks. They tell us the day is not far off when record keeping will be electronic too. Cost is the big bugaboo. Manufacturers and educators are in general agreement that as the quantity of computers goes up cost will go down.

WHAT WILL BE THE ROLE OF THE TEACHER?

If the invention of printing did not replace the teacher it is unlikely that computers will. It is hoped that the teacher will be freed from the grind of endless drill and marking papers—free to counsel, to have time to *listen,* to do research and make plans, to deal with problem children that a machine could never reach. Perhaps the teacher will even have time to build a closer, more personal, more effective relationship with the students.

—— SUMMARY OF AUDIO-VISUAL FACTS ——

Good teachers have always looked for material to make their teaching more effective. To use such material effectively the teacher must know when, and where, and how to use it.

The *still* picture is used when it is impossible to experience the actual situation firsthand. It helps the child doing research to understand his subject more thoroughly.

Be sure the picture used gives the true impression of what you want to emphasize.

The opaque projector magnifies anything that is flat and not larger than 6″ by 6″.

The overhead projector is an improvement over the opaque projector as it eliminates most of the bugs of the latter.

The filmstrip is a simple, effective visual aid, easy to operate, and there is a long list of available filmstrips.

With a bit of practice you and your children can make your own slides to project. The 2″ by 2″ slide can be a simple one of plain or etched glass with a picture painted on it.

A movie can be used to introduce a unit of work, or to enrich it, or to tie together a completed study.

Radio and TV broadcasts are prepared for school children. Although some problems may have to be met and conquered in using them they are excellent aids to you in your teaching.

A tape recorder is an effective way to teach better speech habits. It may be used to good advantage in picking up errors that would go unnoticed in singing or choral speaking. It is invaluable in recording radio programs or some important event in your school.

Taking a field trip or excursion is one of the best means of gaining experience firsthand. It is vitally important to prepare well before the occasion. Discipline is a *must* when out with your class, but it should be the kind of discipline that permits an enjoyable, profitable trip.

Chapter Seven ~

Putting Life into the Teaching
of Music and Art

*E*lementary school teachers sometimes feel that they are expected to be experts in all subjects. In secondary schools the people who teach math, English, science, or health education have been specially trained to do just that and are usually better prepared to teach their own subjects than other members of the staff.

When team teaching becomes established in our schools the person best fitted to teach a particular subject will take on the responsibility for it. Until that goal becomes a reality we shall have to do the best we can with what gifts we possess.

BUT WHAT ABOUT MUSIC AND ART?

Is it possible to do a good job of teaching music and art when you "can't tell one note from another," play no instrument well, are ill at ease with paints and brushes? Can the teacher who's "weak" in those subjects present them to children so that they will get something out of it, something more than "just another lesson?" And is it possible for the teacher who *can* sing a little, or play a little, or can appreciate a work of art, to get children excited, instill in them a love of music and art?

The answer to all these questions is an emphatic "Yes." You *can* teach music and art effectively and profit from the experience at the same time.

MUSIC IS PART OF A CHILD'S LIFE

A baby waves his little arms in the air as he listens to a tune, smiles when a bird sings or his kitten purrs. Then, as a young child, he sings as he plays with toys, taps his foot or fingers in time to music played by a band or to a tune sung by someone in the home.

Primitive tribes beat out rhythms for their ceremonies and discovered that certain reeds gave sweet sounds. Our American Indians performed intricate dances to the beat of the drums. First rhythm and then simple instruments were part of every civilization. And so it is with children—first they experience the joy of keeping time, go on to tunes and songs, and then experiment with instruments.

LET'S START WITH RHYTHM

Someone has called rhythm "the heartbeat of music." The dictionary describes it as "the forward motion of music" and as "harmonious movement." It is certainly born in us for it's almost impossible to resist tapping fingers or feet when we hear the beat of a drum or watch a parade. The kindergarten teacher uses the child's natural sense of rhythm to introduce many new learning games (marching games, singing games, circle games) all involving clapping out the time while they're performed.

PREPARING FOR YOUR RHYTHM BAND

Don't be timid about forming your own classroom rhythm band. It's a good way to start a music program with a new class, and you don't have to know too much about the intricacies of music to succeed. You can use the technique of the kindergarten teacher, adjusting it to the age of your class. Begin with a recording of a lively march as an experiment, and change it quickly to a waltz. You'll find the mood of the children varies with the rhythm of the music. Point out this fact to them and ask them "Why?" Their observations can lead to an interesting discussion.

MAKE YOUR OWN RHYTHM INSTRUMENTS

Children like to experiment with making simple instruments for their rhythm band. If the first try is not completely satisfactory let them vary this or that until the effect produced is what they want. For example:

> *Drum:* A two pound coffee can with both ends removed. Bind both ends tightly and tie fast. Experiment with the effect produced with heavy, strong cloth coated with shellac. Try using pieces of inner tubes. Would it be improved if we used a different kind of can? Smaller? Larger?

> *Drumsticks:* Experiment with short, thick dowels, chair rungs, padded and unpadded drumsticks. Shall we decorate them? Why does the amount of padding change the sound of the "boom!"? (Science lessons on your doorstep with every new question.)

> *Maracas:* Use a glass jar containing beans or a small juice can with pebbles. What would happen if we used a larger container and switched the contents? Someone's father may make you a gift from his produce store— nature's own maraca in the shape of a dried gourd fully equipped with its own handle and rattle.

> *Triangle:* Your rhythm band "triangle" won't be the dainty kind found in the orchestra, for the children will experiment with lengths of metal of several kinds, suspended by a string and struck with another piece of metal, but the sound can be pleasing.

> *Tambourine:* Staple three paper plates together for strength. Sew on eight or ten little dime store bells. Decorate the tambourine as gaudily as you wish; don't forget long, colorful streamers of ribbon.

> *Add cymbals* (which may be nothing more than the right combination of spoon and kettle) and you're ready to try out your band.

TRY THIS TECHNIQUE

You may have a sixth grade that thinks a rhythm band is something for kids. Approach it from a different angle and plan a science unit on musical instruments. Experiment with making some of the simple ones and find out the how and the why for each part of the experiment. Make simple stringed instruments, too, out of anything from cardboard and rubber bands to wood and fine wire, and see if the sound produced can be improved with some care and thought. The proud inventors will want to try out their works of art as they proceed to see if all is going well. First thing you know two or more will try their instruments together, and next thing you know you'll have the makings of a band.

Keep the instruments on display and use them often. Add them to your science-music collection.

WE NEVER OUTGROW RHYTHM BANDS

Playing together in a band, even a rhythm band, is great fun. Whether child or adult, a person with a limited musical background can join others in Mountain Music or Kitchen Bands.

There was a group of women in a retirement community in Florida who, like many retirees, found time heavy on their hands. They joined together to form a Kitchen Band—just for fun at first. Each woman was required to make her own instrument and it's amazing to see how ingenious they were. A funnel became a cornet; a broomstick, a piece of clothesline, and a metal wash-tub became an acceptable bull fiddle. Now the ladies travel all over the home county giving "fun" concerts and they're *good!* I don't know who has more fun—the ladies in the band or the audience they entertain.

Perhaps your class could have such a band.

YOU CAN HAVE SINGING IN THE CLASSROOM

Your class can enjoy group singing right in its own room. You may be afraid to sing out yourself, but you and the children can have a song frequently and even a songfest once in a while. The secret is *well-chosen recordings.*

Take, for example, an album of work song records. They are particularly enjoyable in fifth grade as you study the growth of the nation but can be used for your fourth or sixth grade too. Here again rhythm plays a large role as a child heaves on the anchor chain while he sings a chantey along with the sailors on the ship, or pounds spikes into the railroad ties with the Irish work gang, or thrills to the rhythmic beat of the horse's hoofs as the cowboy rides herd. Try cutting a soft rubber ball in half, cup the halves in your hand, use any hard surface, and you have the perfect sound effect for the pony's feet.

Discuss with your class the many kinds of hard work that were necessary to build a new land and the thrills and dangers connected with such work. Then play a record of a work song. Play it again while the children hum and get the feel of it. Encourage them to sing along with the record. It may sound uncertain and wavery at first, but they'll catch on to the spirit and the rhythm of it quickly, and so will you. It's a satisfaction when they sing and act in rhythm and they'll want to try it again and again.

SPIRITUALS

The long, sad story of slavery needs the songs of the Negro slave to help your children understand the life of these people on the plantations of the Old South. Booker T. Washington said of Negro spirituals, "No race has ever sung so sweetly, or with such perfect charity, while looking forward to the 'year of Jubilo.' " This is the time to tell your class what a song can mean to tired people, how it puts new strength into weary muscles and new hope into a sad heart.

Stories of the Bible were sometimes told to the slaves. Perhaps they heard them from a traveling preacher; perhaps someone on the plantation passed the stories on. They liked to hear about the Children of Israel who had been slaves, too, and they liked to think that another Moses would come and lead them to a promised land. Your record will start with the solo voice so important to the spiritual, "When Israel was in Egypt land," and your children will learn to answer, "Let my people go." It is very impressive and very beautiful.

Your class will enjoy, "Joshua Fit the Battle of Jericho," and encourage them to make all the noise they wish when they sing "And the walls come tumblin' down!"

"He's Got the Whole World in His Hands" will be most effective if you assign one verse to each section of your class, e.g., "He's got you and me, Brother, in His hands," "He's got you and me, Sister, in His hands," "He's got the little bitty baby in His hands," etc., letting each group interpret its part as it wishes, and then everyone sings in unison, "He's got the whole world in His hands."

"Steal Away" and "Nobody Knows" are songs of deep feeling and children love to sing them that way. "Oh, Rock-a My Soul" and "One More River" are not as serious and the boys and girls will feel like letting go on these. There are so many fine spirituals and they're all good! Be sure your class knows that spirituals were not "written" as most songs but came from the hearts of the slaves and were carried from plantation to plantation by the singers themselves.

DOES YOUR SCHOOL HAVE "SONGFESTS"?

Our school has a practice assembly once a week and the period is devoted to singing a few old favorites and to the study of a new song. The repertoire grows quite fast and twice a year we have a festival of song. Each class in the assembly group selects a favorite to sing in the way it chooses. One class may dramatize its selection and another may sing a surprise song practiced behind closed doors. There's some excitement when there is no printed program, and we're not sure what the next class is going to sing until the time comes. There's one person who is in on the secret—the person in charge of the program—but her duties consist mostly of seeing that there are no duplications planned and being the MC.

Another successful type of Sing-o-rama is a Stephen Foster assembly or a Western assembly, both run in much the same way as above.

FIFTH AND SIXTH GRADES ENTERTAIN EACH OTHER

As your fifth grade learns songs about our own country (colonial songs, work songs, patriotic songs) the children may like the idea of an assembly program devoted to the presentation of this music to the sixth grade. The sixth grade can reciprocate by inviting the fifth grade to a program of Pan-American music, or the music of other countries of the world.

In both instances a dance typical of the time and place would be a welcome interlude—a minuet, the Mexican Hat Dance, the Virginia Reel. Both grades can combine their talents to give the third and fourth grades a special treat.

READING MUSIC

You have a set of songbooks in your closet, or perhaps you share several sets in your grade. Comes a time when you admit they should be used. Take one of the books home and get the feel of it. Read the preface—it's there for a reason—and discover the plan of the little music reader. Look through the book to see what you know—there's "America," "Home on the Range," "Swanee River," —and suddenly it doesn't seem so impossible.

As a special treat distribute the books and give your children time to thumb through them. In a few minutes you'll hear half a dozen tunes being hummed. Then a hand goes up, and another. "May we sing 'Down in the Valley'," " 'Clementine'," " 'Au Clair de la Lune'?" Have them sing several songs of their choice. Now it's your turn. You "discover" one (carefully selected beforehand), "All Through the Night," and have the children sing. Then:

1. Talk about the origin of the song, the Welshman's love of singing (in the coal mine, home, and church).

2. "How were we able to read it from the book?" ("I know it." "I can read music." "Anybody can tell if the notes go up or down." "I did just what Nancy did because she's good at singing.")

3. "Suppose we had a new song that no one knows. Where could we start?" While the children talk about staffs and clefs and time signatures hide your surprise. From the fourth year up they have been taught this. Some know it well and others will remember it a bit as the discussion continues. You were probably taught it, too, and find certain terms have a familiar ring.

4. Note well which of the boys and girls seem to know most about reading music. Plan to use their help as you teach a new song or review staffs and signatures. There's nothing underhand about this. They'll enjoy being "teacher" now and then. Just don't shift the responsibility to a child—you're in charge.

5. Study the chart of key signatures that someone left in the back of the closet. Hang it up and plan to use it.

6. A little music reading at a time goes a long way. Beware of letting your class become bored with it. You're out to keep music interesting.

COMPOSING YOUR OWN SONGS

Impossible? No! But "let it happen." There's a certain poem the children love. Try tapping out the rhythm of it with them several times.

"As we tapped out the rhythm of this poem it seemed almost like a song," says the teacher.

Says Peter, "I've been humming some music to myself. Want to hear it?"

The class tries it with Peter's help.

Nancy has an idea of how the music for the next line should go. Then she and Peter teach the two lines to the class. And you're on your way.

Don't try to put the song on the blackboard—not yet, at least. You and they will get bogged down and lose interest. If the attempt at composition is successful ask a more talented coworker to try putting it in black and white, but this is not all-important. The children's creative efforts *are*.

MUSIC APPRECIATION

It's a far cry from the music appreciation classes of some years back to the modern techniques—better records and record players, watching fine orchestral performances on TV and, for many fortunate children, an occasional visit with their class to a beautiful auditorium where they listen to and watch some of the world's finest musicians.

Some of you may remember when music appreciation meant the ability to memorize certain prescribed recordings. Once a year all classes from fifth year up were tested on 10, 15, or 20 of the prescribed selections and there was a great race for the highest average. All kinds of fancy tricks were employed to help the children learn to recognize the records, and, sad to say, few boys and girls knew any part but that which could be played in the first 30 seconds. If the teacher started a record in the middle, or played the end of it instead of the beginning there would be a sea of blank faces staring at her.

It was not a question of appreciating good music and learning to love it or acquiring a taste for it, but simply who had a good memory. Many teachers were unhappy about the situation but this was required work and one had to teach it. Fortunately this is past history for most of us and, usually, we can experiment with music as much as we want to.

UNDERSTANDING THE ORCHESTRA

What a treat to be able to study the composition of an orchestra firsthand instead of from the printed page! How much more it means when a trio, a string quartet, or a band visits your school and the leader introduces the instruments to you. This treat can be arranged. Talk to your music supervisor about the possibility of such a performance in your own auditorium.

ASK FOR HELP IF YOU NEED IT

You will find that your self-confidence grows as you teach music to your class. If a problem comes up that has you stumped, ask another teacher for help. She won't mind, in fact she'll be quite pleased. Perhaps you and she can combine two classes for some lessons, or the other teacher can help you learn a song you want to use but can't get straight. There will be a time when you can repay her, you may be sure of that. And haven't you found that teachers are very willing to lend a hand?

ANYBODY CAN USE THESE TECHNIQUES

Whether you feel that you have little musical ability or feel that you've always had a fair amount of success in teaching the subject, you will find the techniques we have been discussing helpful to you and fascinating to your class. Hold fast to the ideas you have been using *if they work* and try some of the new ones too. Share new ideas with your fellow teachers. As we said in an earlier chapter, "SHARE THE WEALTH!"

No child should be deprived of his heritage of music. There is so much we can give them whether or not we are "gifted." Even the dour Nietzsche said, "Without music, life would be a mistake."

NOW LET'S CONSIDER ART

Children have a right to enjoy art but these lessons can be just as dreary as the wrong kind of music instruction. It's up to you, the teacher, to see that the children in your care receive the best teaching possible. You don't want to deprive them of the pleasures of music and art. *It is important* to overcome your reluctance, to unbend, to enjoy these periods as much as you feel you should. You will have to plan well, do some homework, and be fully prepared. That's true in any area of teaching, but if one feels he's not "gifted" it's doubly important here.

Do you panic when you see small pots of paint, cans of water, an array of brushes? Do you wish you could go into hiding when it's cleanup time? Many of us feel that way but think we have our feelings hidden. Unfortunately, the results betray us.

We have a choice—to go on dreading art periods and fumbling through each one somehow or *facing the problem squarely and doing something constructive about it.*

You want to do something about it? Good!

1. **Become acquainted** with the room in which most of your art lessons will take place:

(a) Where are paints, brushes, crayons, etc., stored?

(b) Is there a plentiful supply of newspapers to protect desks?

(c) What provision has been made for the easy distribution of paints and brushes, crayons, pastels?

(d) If there is no sink in the room what plan has been devised for a supply of water for painting and cleanup?

(e) How many easels are available? How will you have them used for best results?

(f) Are there some good pictures on the walls? Samples of children's work too?

If painting and other art lessons take place in your own room there are certain advantages. First and most important is the fact that you can plan the mechanics of your art periods the way you prefer. If you use the "art room" you must follow the regulations set up there for the convenience of all classes. Another advantage of using your own classroom is the freedom to have the lesson when the class is ready and anxious for it. Here you have the flexibility that is of such importance in the sustaining of interest in a subject (emphasized in Ch. 3 on Planning). The children reach a point where their hands are itching to put a picture on paper. If you have to say, "When we're in the art room next Tuesday we'll do such and such . . ." there won't be much enthusiasm now or then.

2. **Become acquainted** with the materials the children use:

(a) Practice in private the manipulation of paint brushes large and small. Paint with water on a large surface such as the blackboard until your hand gets the feel of the brush and you're not afraid to sweep across the surface from one side to the other.

(b) Tape a sheet of newsprint on the board. Brush on plenty of water. Take a primary color and a large brush and cover the surface with paint. Let it spread. Take another primary color and as you brush it on watch it blend with the first.

It's a pleasant experience isn't it? Now you begin to see why children of all ages like to "mess around" with paints. There's a sort of relaxation and a letting go connected with them.

(c) Practice mixing paints. Can you mix the secondary colors so necessary to a picture? Have you tried varying the amounts used to obtain shades of these colors?

(d) Keep all your practice paintings large and fill the paper with the picture. (Encourage the children to do the same.)

You don't have to be an artist to give your class these opportunities for relaxation and pleasure any more than you need to be a musician to help your class enjoy music.

3. **Become acquainted** with the basic procedures necessary in painting:

(a) Practice cleaning the brushes you used. How will you have the children do it when the room is full?

(b) What will you do with the unused paints? What will the children do with their unused paints? You *must* have this planned in advance.

(c) What does one do with a wet picture? You can't hang it on the wall.

These "become acquainted" hints are absolutely necessary. There will be bedlam unless you plan seriously beforehand and practice in private. Most of these problems will have to be solved by *you,* for you are the one who knows not only what material and accommodations are available but where the art lessons will be given and what the arrangements are in your school.

You might also ask the old hands what they do. Their rooms and storage space may be similar to yours, or they may share with you a good practical device for the distribution and collection of materials. If you are a new teacher, or just beginning to gain some confidence in your ability to teach a painting lesson, ask your supervisor for permission to watch someone give such a lesson. Notice how *she* has solved some of the knotty problems of distribution and cleanup. What does *she* do with wet, dripping paintings? Leave them on the desks to dry? Put them on the floor?

NOW THAT YOU HAVE SOME CONFIDENCE

Look upon teaching art in the same practical way you look at modern math. When that program began in your school district, what did you do? It would have been useless to wring your hands and bemoan the fact that this was new and strange to you. You faced it as part of the job and you had to master it. You took in-service courses, observed district math coordinators teach your class, read pertinent material, learned the new language of modern math, perhaps even sent away for a set of records you thought might help. You managed to stay ahead of your class so you could still be the guide, and you succeeded, and you never considered yourself a mathematician either.

Apply the same determination to the teaching of art. You may never paint a masterpiece but you can guide children in the enjoyment of the many forms of art. The secret lies in the fact that a teacher prepares for an art lesson with the same careful thought given to a social studies unit, a new concept in math, or the teaching of a folk dance.

BEFORE YOUR CLASS PAINTS

If your class is a fourth, fifth, or sixth grade it would be a good idea to discuss with the children the need for a definite set of rules for getting the most out of a painting lesson. Encourage them to talk about past experiences with brushes, paint, and cleanup. As they talk make mental notes. Are there signs of careless habits that will have to be corrected? Does Ronnie have a good plan for preparing material? If you're not sure the ideas are practical, try them out—in private, of course. Take, for example, the suggestion that cardboard egg cartons hold small amounts of enough colors for a group of four or six painters. See if it works. Does the paint seep through? Or is it the perfect answer?

When the rules and regulations have been agreed upon, tape them in a conspicuous place near the supply closet. Now the children can show you how much they know about preparing for a painting lesson by actually going through the motions, first with water and large brushes. If this is successful take the primary colors in the next lesson and see how they clean up. If it's obvious that the class needs more practice, give it to them. It will mean a great deal to you and be more enjoyable for them if they are well trained before tackling a regular painting period.

NOW—SHALL WE PAINT?

There are times when children paint anything they wish, and there will be many times when everyone is painting the same subject with each child interpreting it in his own way. Let's say your first or second graders are painting anything they wish about the circus, or the family, or their own classroom. Your results may vary from a clown to a circus tent, from a pet kitten to an apartment house, from a picture of "Teacher" to a favorite library book.

Older children might take the subject of Thanksgiving and paint the Pilgrim Fathers with their blunderbusses, or a turkey farm, or a family gathered around the table. You will find that each child interprets the subject differently according to his experience and background.

If you are painting murals to illustrate a project be sure to provide a variety of research pictures or films to give your class the opportunity to see many examples of Indian life, Norsemen's ships, musical instruments, the natives or the cities of Brazil—

whatever your unit of work may be. Sometimes we forget how limited is the background and vocabulary of many children. The more variety you can present to them the more imaginative are the results.

SEIZE UNUSUAL OPPORTUNITIES

That first snow! Do you remember how excited you were at the age of seven, or nine, or eleven when the first flakes of winter fell? Forget your rather jaundiced attitude toward snow for the moment and let the children go to the windows and watch it. Would they like to paint? If you are in the middle of a reading or math lessons, forget it. There's always tomorrow for reading and math, but the snow will be melted or black with soot and traffic by that time and you can finish the math then.

Suppose there's a moon launching on TV. Let them paint. Children's imaginations run riot at a time like this and you may get some weird effects.

The home team wins the series! Will they paint their baseball hero, or the stadium, or will it be something you would never think of?

A visit to the firehouse or a walk in the park—children will immortalize it on paper. Take such opportunities for painting and your class will always associate art with something that gives pleasure.

FINGER PAINTING

Small children love finger painting. The surface is large and the paint good and slippery, and no one says, "What a mess!" See that each child has put on (backwards) an old short-sleeved shirt that Daddy has discarded. Provide some finger paints and cover things with loads of newspaper. The artists start by putting a little puddle of water on the shiny side of the paper—then you stand back and watch them get rid of some frustrations in an acceptable way, and have fun too.

Although children in higher grades still enjoy finger painting they seldom get the opportunity. You will find that with some guidance they can produce unexpected surrealist effects by using the side of the hand instead of fingers or palm, and by painting one design on top of another. If you are going to have finger painting in fourth to sixth grades it would be wise to practice (in private, again), so that you will be acquainted with problems that may arise from attempts at surrealism. You will be in a position to suggest effects or colors suitable to such attempts.

LEFTOVER CRAYONS

Miss Francis insists upon a neat supply closet. She stayed after school one day to sort and weed out her art supplies with the assistance of Kathy, the monitor. They piled up quite a stack of crayon bits—odds and ends of all colors.

"Do you know what my sister would do with these?" said Kathy. "She makes flowers, designs sort of, but they're pretty."

"However in the world does she do that?" asked Miss Francis, on the lookout for a new idea.

Well, it seems that Kathy's sister is quite artistic for a 12-year-old. She shaves the little pieces and lets them fall on a paper and arranges them casually as flowers. Then she covers her "flowers" with a paper and presses them with a warm iron. A little brush and some paint connect the floral shapes with leaves and stems—and presto!—an interesting design!

Miss Francis has a new idea to try with her class (after she experiments in private).

PUPPETS ARE FASCINATING

Puppets and marionettes have been entertaining audiences for untold centuries. Even early civilizations have left evidence that the delightful little creatures entertained them too. We're still charmed and intrigued by them and lose ourselves willingly to the show on the miniature stage.

Have you ever been able to take your eyes from the performance long enough to see the effect of such a show on children? They are spellbound! Yet how they can laugh or suffer with the puppets as the story progresses! Being children they, too, want to have their own puppets and put on their own show. If they are overly ambitious and want to build and maneuver marionettes they will find it takes a long while to acquire that much skill. Use *your* skills as a teacher to persuade them that they can have more fun with the simpler kinds of puppets.

PAPER PUPPETS

Children of any grade enjoy making paper puppets and performing with them. Often it's no more than a paper bag with a crayon drawing for a face, but they can become quite elaborate when the owner staples on ears, nose, mouth, and some woolen hair. A child can learn to manipulate the paper bag puppet by pulling the bag over his hand and squeezing it around his wrist. It's surprising how real it can look when a little play is being acted out with characters like these.

Puppets made of paper and stuffed with rags or cotton can be mounted on sticks and maneuvered from behind a screen. A shy child is delighted to make a puppet out of himself by devising a sort of mask from a paper bag and slipping it over his head. How quickly his shyness disappears behind this disguise, and how much more readily he contributes to the dialogue of the play.

Then there is the paper puppet that has identical front and rear views. Its head, arms, and legs are cut out separately and attached with clips. A child learns to move the head or arm independently which makes for more realistic drama. A lion moves its head as it roars; a cat swishes its tail. Mounted on sticks and moved from behind a screen or curtain they can be lots of fun.

PUPPETS CAN BE ELABORATE TOO

There are so many kinds of puppets. There's the papier-mâché head requiring time and patience and some skill, the "sock" puppet that can be dressed up and decorated with buttons and bows, the "finger" puppet that can become as sweet and dainty as its young creator wishes.

USE YOUR PUPPETS

Making puppets is a delightful art experience and so is the construction of stages and background scenery and the sewing of the tiny clothes. But the same puppets can be used effectively with your other studies. Take, for example, language arts. What more acceptable way could be found to correct common grammatical errors, teach good manners, present a book report or original poetry, than speaking through one's little puppet friends? Writing short dialogues, learning the graces of conversation, acting, good voice control are much more fun with puppets.

Your social studies will take on new meaning when the tiny figures venture out into the New World. Teach a new song through a puppet or let a sweet singer who is too shy to appear in public perform behind a goodnatured puppet. There is no end to the ways in which they may be used.

DIORAMAS

Before your class tries to make dioramas there should be many opportunities to study and closely examine some more professional examples, such as the ones you borrow from a museum. These three-dimensional "pictures" are very lifelike and children are interested in studying them and in trying to make their own.

Ideally, a diorama is a group project. Keep the group down to four, six at the most, or you'll find more argument than progress. Let's say that your class has been studying pioneer life and as a culmination of this project plans to make a semipermanent exhibit. One group may want a Boonesboro exhibit, another an Indian attack on a wagon train, and a third will plan an evening campfire on the trail. Perhaps you can encourage a fourth group to display the interior of a cabin with mother cooking at the hearth. There will have to be a few unattached individuals to make the background mountain scenery and do whatever printing is necessary. Someone will prefer to be the research authority rather than being attached to any particular group.

The girls who are sewing the clothes and devising the types of dolls to wear them will enjoy working together no matter what group they're from. The boys who are building tiny palisades or cabins or wagons can lend a hand to each other or make suggestions to speed along the project. In this way you have a united class effort even as your individual groups are preparing separate dioramas.

If all this sounds too elaborate for the class you have in mind try a diorama of cutouts of paper dolls, paper or cardboard furnishings, wagons—whatever you like.

YOU'LL WANT TO TRY THESE

As you progress in your teaching of art and gain confidence in your ability to try new things, see what can be done with weaving

—with colored paper, bright wool, raffia. See how your children develop skill in clay modeling. Let their imaginations take over as they experiment with collage and mobiles. You can keep your room bright and interesting, a room teacher and children are proud of, something that you and they have created with hard work, loving care, and a great deal of satisfaction.

GUIDING YOUR CLASS IN THE APPRECIATION OF GREAT ART

Use stories of famous painters and sculptors as part of your reading program. There are fine biographies for reading pleasure or for book reports for the 10- to 12-year-old group.

If there are art galleries and museums in your city plan to visit them. First, go there alone so you can plan what you want your children to study and be able to avoid the weariness and boredom too often associated with this kind of excursion. If a guide is available for your trip let him know in advance what you want the class to see. Is it American artists of the Colonial period? English? Flemish? Italian? Don't try too much at one time!

Museums often have fine little prints of great paintings which can be bought reasonably. The children can make attractive frames for these and you will have your own classroom gallery of art.

—— YOU DON'T HAVE TO BE "GIFTED" ——

Teaching music and art can present problems to the person who feels she's not "gifted," but there are many ways in which these subjects can be made interesting and profitable to teacher and students.

"Rhythm is the heartbeat of music" and we start with that.

Children can make and play their own simple rhythm instruments—drum, cymbals, tambourine, maracas, triangle.

Older children may be approached from the scientific angle with a unit on musical instruments. This might possibly develop into a Kitchen Band.

Use carefully selected recordings of work songs such as chanteys, railroad and cowboy songs. Your class sings with the record and acts out the rhythm.

"Spirituals" are very effective when the solo voice and chorus are used.

A good way to get children singing enthusiastically in large groups is to have a songfest once in a while. Here they can entertain each other with songs they have learned in the assemblies or in the classroom.

If you plan and prepare ahead you and your class can read music from songbooks. Start with some familiar ones. Use the assistance of pupils who take lessons and can read music. It's not too impossible to compose music starting with a familiar poem that has a good rhythmic beat.

To further the children's appreciation of good music choose your recordings carefully; encourage your class to watch certain TV programs; take them to a concert, if possible; try to have musicians visit your assemblies.

Ask fellow teachers and supervisors for help if you need it.

Conquer your fear of paints, brushes, and cleanups by practicing in private with the equipment used in classroom painting lessons.

Plan each part of your lesson making sure that you are familiar with what the children will do and the problems that can arise.

Discuss with your class the need for definite rules about preparing for and cleaning up after an art lesson.

Each child interprets a subject according to his experience and background. Since many children have little of either provide them with as many pictures or films as possible.

Seize the opportunity to paint when interest is high. Don't postpone it.

As your confidence grows try puppets, dioramas, clay modeling, collage, mobiles. You can keep your room bright and attractive and your class will learn to associate art with pleasure.

Chapter Eight

Building
Responsibility in Children

CAN A TEACHER INSTILL A SENSE OF RESPONSIBILITY IN CHILDREN?

Let's face it! You can't instill a sense of responsibility in your children *unless you know the meaning of it yourself!* Only as a teacher assumes his own responsibilities is he able to build responsibility in others.

TWO KINDS OF TEACHERS

Suppose we have a look at two kinds of teachers who can be found in almost any school. Mrs. Bishop has years of experience, years that have molded her into a good teacher. She's made her share of mistakes but tries not to repeat them. She herself works hard and expects a good deal from her children. They like and respect her. It's a break to inherit one of her well-trained classes.

Across the hall is Miss Carson—young, cute, and undisciplined. Mrs. Bishop tried to take the girl under her wing and give her the benefit of her own hard-won experience. It was unappreciated and ignored. The young teacher complains that her class never settles down to work until 10 AM. The children's books are uncovered, their papers carelessly written. When the class passes down the hall all work has to stop in the rooms along the line of march. And they're fresh!

Mrs. Bishop arrives 20 to 30 minutes ahead of her class. Two monitors go upstairs with her and dust, wash boards, and straighten up the library. When the class arrives their room is ready.

The door to Miss Carson's room is closed and the shades still drawn as they were yesterday to keep out the bright afternoon sun. Boards are chalky, books lie all over the desks and windowsills. When the children arrive at the closed door they push each other around until Mrs. Bishop leaves her own group to get her neighbor's class out of the hall and into their own room. After three or four trips back and forth she sees Miss Carson sauntering down the hall, calm and beautiful after a session in front of the rest room mirror.

Mrs. Bishop remarks irritably that she's tired of this daily baby-sitting. Miss Carson shrugs and she will tell anyone who will listen that Mrs. Bishop is an old pill and should retire.

The young teacher is bright enough. She's not pleased with the way things are going, and she has good reason to know that her principal is not pleased either. But she won't make the effort required to correct the situation. She'll muddle through the year and pass her class on to someone else—you, perhaps.

WHERE DO YOU START WITH SUCH A CLASS?

Scolding and nagging will get you nowhere. Children are always being scolded or nagged and they don't even hear it at this stage of the game. Save your energy for something more productive. What I am about to recommend is not easy but it will pay big dividends to you and to these children you must face for a year!

TEN POINT PLAN FOR FIRMING UP YOUR CLASS

1. State your immediate problem *in writing: (This is vitally important.)*

   I have a class of 31 children, 10 and 11 years old. They have come to me careless in habits of work, dress, and speech. When I ask them a question I receive a "Yeah" or a "Nah" answer. They have little respect for me and none for their school or schoolwork.

   There are five, possibly more, who seem to be made of sterner stuff, but they have fallen into bad habits as members of the class.

   Homework is largely ignored. Those who bring it in are almost ashamed to have even partially fulfilled an assignment. I say "partially" because the work is so carelessly done it is worth little.

I have given the problem much thought in the week and a half the class has been with me. I can't go on in this manner. I have considered the possibility of discussing the situation with the children, but if it didn't work out I'd be worse off than before.

If only I had planned more carefully when I knew this group was coming to me, but I didn't bother. If I had shown them that I meant business that first morning!

Where can I start?

(Congratulations! You *have* started. You have made yourself sit down and face the problem. You know the "ifs" and "buts" are behind you. You realize that you have an uphill battle on your hands. It is important that you do not attempt to remake the class in a day or in a month. Plan *one* line of attack at a time, and be sure it is working satisfactorily before you undertake more ambitious measures.)

2. Stay after school today. Take a good look at your room. Pretty drab? You haven't had the urge to fix it up—too worn out and discouraged? Wash the board. Throw out the plants that died of neglect. Put some books that *look* interesting and *are* interesting on your windowsills. Dust the library table and put some attractive books on it and just *two* chairs nearby.

   Throw out the junk on your own desk and leave a few businesslike books there instead. You can tackle the cluttered drawers tomorrow afternoon because you're you're not going to make that early bus for a long time.

   Take a look at your plan book. If the children handed you something like this you'd be insulted. You will need careful planning from here on. Take it home with you tonight (if this is heresy use looseleaf paper) and write out your plan for tomorrow *in detail*.

3. Arrange your home schedule so that you will be able to get home later and leave earlier until a brighter day dawns. *This is important for your peace of mind* because your working days will be longer and harder than ever, and you must have your home problems taken care of.

4. You have begun to assume responsibility for these children in your care. That is the core of the problem. Type or print the following quotation from John Dewey's * *Individualism, Old and New* and keep it where you will see it and reread it every day:

"There can be no stable or balanced development of mind and character apart from the assumption of responsibility."

5. Leave home in plenty of time. This is no morning to rush in breathless. Look around your room. Is there something more you can do to help that vital first 10 minutes? Clear away the old posters and books from the wardrobe shelf. Do you know exactly how you will have the children put away coats? (Be glad it's not raining, that's a break!)

6. *Be at the door when your class comes up from the yard,* but do not permit anyone to enter the room. This is what you should have done the first day, but there's no time now for regrets. Walk up and down the line with a word or a look of praise for those who have caught on to the idea that something new has started. Ask any showoffs to step to one side. The element of surprise is working with you. Don't overdo it by keeping them out in the hall too long. Send in a few at a time to put away coats, but take a position that allows you to see what's going on.

7. Don't spoil the effect by talking; they're dying to know what's going to happen. Keep them guessing; it will occupy their attention temporarily. Give very few, very simple orders. Have the flag salute, but wait for good, respectful posture. It's pretty hard for a child in an American school to resist coming to attention at this time. They expect to sing the national anthem next. Don't push your luck. That can wait for another morning.

8. This was your one special technique planned for today. Do the same thing *every* morning. *This is important.* You will very gradually establish a pattern for these children to follow. It will give you all a sense of responsibility.

---

* *Individualism, Old and New,* John Dewey, Minton Balch & Co.

9. Without any explanation, without permitting any questions to be asked, without raising your voice once, assign some simple quiet work and walk around and supervise it. Don't permit anyone to leave his seat while the assignment is being carried out. At the end of a reasonable length of time have them mark their own papers under your direction. Go around and collect them *yourself* and tell the children in a quiet, even voice that you will recheck the papers, record the marks, and return them tomorrow morning. (There will be a few children who will have second thoughts about the paper they have just handed you, but that's probably just what they need to start the straightening out process.)

10. You have taken yourself in hand, and you have made the first beginnings toward creating a sense of responsibility in the children. It doesn't show yet, but a seed has been sown. Refrain from talking more than is absolutely necessary. This impresses children and you will see them looking at you and wondering. Let them wonder. You are building slowly and now you have two blocks in place. That's enough for today. Don't try too much. Keep your voice low; have them do familiar, simple work. Plan tonight what the next strategy will be. You *may* try it tomorrow and you *may* have to wait. Your class will let you know when you meet them at the door. Perfect that operation first.

RESPONSIBILITY BUILDS CHARACTER

You are smart enough to know that you can never teach personal responsibility to children unless you have first disciplined yourself. Already your class has sensed a change in you—there is a firmness and quietness that has impressed them and calmed them down. Children are uncanny in sensing any sign of strength or weakness in adults. The new security that the class begins to feel will work two ways. You as the teacher will want to do more for them and with them. Your pupils will be more attentive, more receptive, and will start to take pride in their group and in themselves.

Beware of moving too fast! Plan every new move in detail. Picture yourself and the class doing this new thing you're thinking about. Picture how some of the more difficult children might react to it, and whether the group is ready to take that step. You can't afford to fail for you might lose precious ground already gained. Build slowly and solidly, always remembering that these children have had little discipline and guidance for the past year and you can't expect them to change overnight.

In writing down your problem you stated that there were several who seemed to be made of sterner stuff than the rest. Start to give them the opportunity to serve in some small way. Ask Jeanne if she would like to fix up the bulletin board. Tell her you have some pictures and clippings she may use. She is delighted and wants to know if Marian can work with her. Get out the block letters and let them try a heading for the top of the bulletin board.

Without seeming to, notice how the class is reacting to this, and if it's wise to start another monitor on a job. Resist the temptation to offer Jack a bribe in the form of any kind of position. See how he is trying to attract your attention. Ignore him. When you're ready you know whom you'll try out for the board-washing job— and it isn't Jack.

Delegate small assignments in responsibility, two children here, one child there. Watch and see how they are accepting the challenge. Insist quietly on a job well done. Don't be above helping them if they are willing but not too adept, and don't permit any careless, half-done performance.

WHAT ABOUT GROUP WORK?

There are many kinds of group work. Forget most of them until you know you have the class in hand. My own experience has been that the dividing of such a class into reading or math groups would, at this stage, be a mistake. They would learn nothing and your control might be lost. There will always be one parent who will hotfoot it to the principal demanding to know why a teacher in his school uses such antediluvian methods of nongrouping instruction. If he's a good supervisor he will not only accept your reasons but will be thankful you used your head.

Confine your groups temporarily to monitorial work, just two or three children in each, and supervise them carefully. Such groups can keep the classroom library in order, take the responsibility for taking care of the new plants, arrange a very elementary science exhibit, make a chart for recording daily temperatures. You may feel you have to work with your four worst readers. Make sure the rest of the class has a simple assignment that *they know you are going to correct.* I say "simple" because you don't want them acting up or interrupting you while you're working with this little reading group. Fifteen or 20 minutes is long enough for an assignment now.

Keep all your periods short, much as you would do with younger children. As your ability to hold their attention strengthens you can lengthen such periods of work a bit at a time. Vary your studies so that you give the class a reading lesson, math, some kind of social studies that does not call for grouping, language arts. Plan games to break up the monotony of lessons—games that may involve numbers, names of cities and countries, a simple "What's My Name?" history game. This will require detailed planning on your part, but when you see your class gradually turning into a manageable group of children you will be well repaid.

READ GOOD STORIES TO YOUR CHILDREN

Read to your class. Try them out on stories of heroes and heroines. Avoid making too big a point of the heroes' 100 per cent goodness—some of the children might reject them permanently.

Talk about the hero and encourage your young audience to discuss him. Find out what appeals to your class. What might they have done in his situation? Wasn't that a big responsibility for a boy? How would your girls like to have so many jobs to do helping their pioneer parents?

Make such stories available. Tell them you're putting certain books on the library table; hold them up and show them. There are excellent biographies for 10-year-olds. Ask your school or town librarian for suggestions. You'll feel good when first one child and then another starts reading on his own. Who can tell what fine traits may rub off on them? Children are going to worship heroes of one kind or another—try to provide them with the right kind.

WHEN CAN THEY ASSUME MORE RESPONSIBILITY?

There will come a day when you'll be able to have discussions with your class about school affairs. They may want to talk over the possibility of electing their own class president or G.O. representatives. By this time you should know whether or not they are ready to assume so much responsibility. Use your good judgment.

Don't permit yourself to be pushed into a situation that you can't handle. Let them assume small responsibilities and when they prove themselves in these permit them to go on to bigger things.

This carefully planned, one-step-at-a-time technique for dealing with a difficult class can be used with satisfying results in a so-called underprivileged neighborhood. These children suffer frequently from the lack of firm guidance and from the feeling that no one cares. The deliberately slow building of confidence and mutual respect is a new experience for many of them.

THE TEACHER'S EXAMPLE IS ALL-IMPORTANT

Children will copy a teacher's way of speaking, her hairdo, facial expressions, and her manners too. It can be disconcerting to see a careless slipup of our own come home to roost in our classroom. Miss Mason, for example, insisted on courteous behavior from her class at all times. When she had difficulty making one class of hers act the way she expected them to in the auditorium she decided to talk with them and find the reason.

As the discussion progressed, she noticed a reluctance on the part of the children to talk up. Finally her class president said, "Miss Mason, you tell us to be very polite in the assembly hall and to give our attention to what is going on during the program. But——but you——," (here he hesitated) "whenever we have a movie——you go to the back of the auditorium——and you——you talk and laugh with Mrs. Simmons——and we don't think that's fair!"

THE TEACHER'S RESPONSIBILITY TO MARK WORK

We expect our pupils to have assigned work ready on time. If you are in the habit of giving a weekly contract (in spelling, for example) you write it carefully on the board and expect them to copy it. You give a little checkup test during the week as a warning to get busy, and on Friday morning you collect the contract. That's good training in individual responsibility. *But when do you return such an assignment to your pupils?*

Suppose you teach a new step in a math problem. Then, wanting to find out if the children understand the new work, you test them. But how good *are you* at getting the papers marked and returned? They want to know the results of a test and have every right to get their papers back while interest is still keen. You are busy, in school and out, and time slips by. So does the interest of the children. This is true of all aspects of schoolwork. For example if you wait too long to return book reports your comments and suggestions lose all freshness, all connection with the coaching in written expression you've been giving them.

In order to teach children to respect an assignment and to assume the responsibility of having it ready on time *you* must show them that it's important enough to be marked, returned, and discussed with them in the shortest possible time.

NOBODY LIKES TO CHECK PAPERS

Marking papers is a chore. It is time-consuming and frequently boring. Can you think of anything less inspiring than a set of book reports from a slow class? But the job has to be faced. Perhaps the paper you hold and dread to begin work on represents the best that Helen can do. She may have worried through her book and tried hard to please you—and this is it! She's a sweet kid and you don't want to hurt her. Why not try this and see how it works?

Write on her paper: "Helen, can you and I have a talk about this report? Please come to see me today after the library period begins." You won't have to spend so much time making corrections and changes on her paper. The child would never understand them anyway. Talking with her will be pleasanter for both of you.

Here's another hint you may find helpful. You've given your class a quiz in fractions. It's rather new work and you want to know if they understand it. Take a sampling of the papers, just pull out five or six without looking at the names. If you find many errors return all the papers. Tell the class you think it will be helpful if you go over the work together, each marking his own paper, and talk about the mistakes. The next day give a similar quiz. It will be easier to mark and to judge how they stand in that type of work.

Once in a great while you may have to give your class an unexpected assignment (perhaps you are called to the office and someone is minding the group for you) and you don't plan to mark the papers. Just "file them away" in a corner of your own coat closet. Don't "file" them in your neighbor's wastebasket where her moni-

tor will find them and feel honor bound to tell *your* children
what he found.

KEEPING PROMISES

This has to work both ways! If you promise your class *anything,*
whether it is a reward or a punishment, *see it through.* They will
think more highly of you if you punish them when they truly deserve it than they will if you soften after the anger has passed and
let them off with a warning. So be wary of threats, for people often
make dire threats in a careless moment and then worry about getting off the hook without losing face. This puts a teacher in a bad
position. Our school lives are complicated enough without adding
problems of our own making.

Let the children know that you expect *them* to keep a promise
too. Having work ready on time is part of their responsibility and
a very important part of promise-keeping. Discourage loose promises. Children will tell you they can bring such-and-such an article
for exhibit and then discover mother won't let it out of her sight—
it's a family heirloom.

With most classes you can discuss promises, especially the kinds
of promises that are frequently made between children and
teacher. Emphasize the fact that assignments are promises too. If
one child is a monitor who meets you each morning and comes up
early to help prepare the classroom, he is expected to be there.
When a child is responsible for any job for a day, for a month
insist that it be well done *without your nagging.* Part of his promise is to take care of the job without the teacher having to follow
him up.

Discuss also the fact that sometimes people are sick and are unable to keep their word and be where they are expected. What
happens then? Children like to talk about such matters and it
further points up the importance of a promise.

DISCUSSION OF GROUP PROBLEMS ENCOURAGES RESPONSIBILITY

When the rapport between teacher and pupils is good most
problems can be settled by talking them out. This is not advisable
unless you know your group and they like and respect you. (Problems involving one child, even if all are affected, should not come
up for public airing.)

Mr. Klein has a sixth grade. He is the teacher in charge of visual aids, and when a movie is to be shown in the assembly he takes his monitors down 10 minutes early to prepare the film, close shades, etc. Miss Brady across the hall keeps an eye on Mr. Klein's class, takes them down to the auditorium, brings them back, and watches them until he returns. That's quite an order when you realize that she has her own group to supervise too!

All has gone well until recently. Now Miss Brady is beginning to complain that the line is too long and she can't be at both ends of it. She should be able to rely on Mr. Klein's children to behave in the halls but they don't. There's pushing and giggling and running to catch up. The two teachers are good neighbors and have talked it over privately. It is Mr. Klein's idea to have Miss Brady voice the complaint to him in front of the class. Then he will ask the president to take charge of the discussion that is sure to follow. He (the teacher) will be there to supervise and guide if needed. Such a problem can usually be settled this way and make everyone concerned happy. How much better it is to appeal to the sense of responsibility in children than to resort to scolding and threats!

PAINTING PROBLEM IN THE THIRD GRADE

Mrs. Grand's third graders love to paint, but the resulting mess in the room is awful. The teacher feels that these children are too young to come up with a solution so she plans to change the procedure of the art lessons. But she will have her class talk about the problem of cleaning up after painting, and she will lead the discussion around to the change she has in mind.

THIS IS MRS. GRAND'S PLAN

Instead of having a painting lesson for all the children at the same time she will set up two easels in the back of the classroom. A small table will hold the necessary cans of water, the paints, and the brushes. While the greater part of the class has a drawing, weaving, or clay modeling period, four children will work at the easels. There will be a schedule printed so every child will know just when his painting privilege is coming. Then each of the four will be responsible for the necessary cleanup of painting utensils and other paraphernalia and for preparing for the artist who is to follow him.

Mrs. Grand found that this worked better than the old hit-and-miss method. The painting lessons were more fruitful and the room was kept clean. Each small child learned that his job of cleaning up his own brushes contributed something important to his class.

John Dewey, who understood human nature at its best and worst, said, "Only by sharing in some responsible task does there come a fitness to share in it." *

REMEMBERING OUR OWN RESPONSIBILITY
—— WHEN TEACHING IT TO CHILDREN ——

Only as a teacher assumes his own responsibilities is he able to instill responsibility in others.

If you inherit an untrained, irresponsible class it is up to you to start from scratch. Begin with yourself, stating your problem *in writing*, and plan a slow, careful campaign, correcting one phase of the problem before you attempt another.

A quiet firmness is effective in handling children who lack discipline and responsibility.

Well-chosen stories of famous people followed by class discussion of them will give children an idea of what responsibility means.

Children watch and imitate the teacher. Be sure you don't give them a bad example to copy.

Marking the children's work promptly is the responsibility of the teacher. Show them that you consider the assignment important enough to be checked.

Sometimes a little talk with a poor student is more effective than much criticism of his written work.

Keep your promises to the children if you expect them to keep their's.

Most group problems can be talked over with the class. It encourages them to feel a responsibility for their solution.

---

* "Democracy in Education" in the *Elementary School Teacher*, IV, 1903.

Effective Handling of Bright
and Slow Children

$\mathcal{O}$ne of the most pressing problems in teaching is how to deal competently with the two extremes of the class: those who move faster than the majority and those who can't keep up. Since the curriculum is prepared with the great majority of children in mind those who fit into this large middle group present no *unusual* problem.

We have always known that a few children possess outstanding ability, but using this ability to the best advantage takes some doing. The bright child finishes an assignment before his neighbor finds a pencil. What will we do with him? Give him more examples or more sentences to write? A poor way to reward competence! Perhaps he can do some special research for the class or help a bewildered neighbor with math or spelling. He can do almost anything you ask of him, but how much is it fair to ask? Are you using his ability to the best advantage? Unless you handle him wisely such a child becomes bored or develops into a disciplinary problem.

HAS INTELLIGENCE TESTING BEEN THE ANSWER?

A good many years ago there was tremendous interest in finding the IQ of every child. The original idea was good. Something must be done to prevent the all too obvious waste of intelligence. If the plan could have been carried out the way the French psychologist, Alfred Binet, originally planned, it might have been a boon to mankind. However, when hundreds or thousands of children were involved the Binet Test was impracticable. So it was changed and watered down through the years until the result was a series of shorter tests given to the class as a group and totaling about 45 minutes time. Instead of being administered by a trained psychologist, the intelligence test was given by a teacher who might or might not have had any instruction in the handling of so important an assignment. To make the IQ rating obtained more meaningful some school systems gave each child three such tests during the elementary years.

THE SACROSANCT IQ

At last we had the answer—or so we thought. Now we would be able to separate these bright youngsters from those who held them back. There would be no more of this heterogeneous grouping for we would have classes for the bright, classes for the Great Majority, classes devoted to the instruction of the slow. Each little individual was now labeled, perhaps for life, and what method had we used? Why, the Intelligence Test, of course. Was there any better way?

Here and there a voice was heard crying in the wilderness; now and then a protest was made against such an autocratic way of consigning the Great Majority to mediocrity, but to little or no avail. The IQ swept the country. Teachers were counseled against divulging a child's IQ to the parents who had a very natural curiosity about the subject. Let's look at the way this wave of IQ consciousness affected: (1) child, (2) teacher, (3) parent.

1—THE CHILD AND HIS IQ LABEL

Some children do well on tests and some don't. It's not always the slow child who shows up in a poor light on such an occasion. A few become so nervous they can't function properly. Others don't read or listen to the directions given them. (A sign of lack of intelligence? Not necessarily.) Still others become so involved with one part of the test they don't want to leave it unfinished and proceed to the next.

A child may not feel well on the day of the test, or he may have had an unfortunate start that morning. Test him three times in his elementary school career if you will, but if there is one low score on his IQ record there will always be some doubt about the accuracy of the other two.

Then we have countless children who suffer from their background. They are called underprivileged for several reasons such as a language barrier or unsavory home conditions. What kind of result have we any right to expect of them? Must they be considered dull or even borderline because of some handicap that lowers their IQ rating but not their inherent intelligence?

2—THE TEACHER AND THE IQ

When a teacher has a class of 25 to 35 and tries to set up a system of grouping that will be fair and workable, the IQ on the record card looms large. We have been told by the experts to use it as a guide. What teacher who sees a 132 IQ on Billy's card is going to put him in a slow or even a medium reading group. But if David's IQ is 99 the chances are that *he* will go to the medium group, and even then there may be some doubt as to whether or not he can handle middle group reading.

The teacher who had some misgivings about the infallibility of the IQ was considered outmoded. This was especially true a few years ago before the pendulum started to swing back. Now we find that some of the largest school systems in the country have backed away from the idea and have come to the conclusion that the IQ is sometimes unreliable and unfair.

3—THE PARENT AND THE IQ

It is natural for parents to feel that their child is unusual, and if there is anything that makes a parent bristle it is the thought that his child's ability is not fully appreciated. IQ scores opened up a whole new field of potential friction between the parent and the school. The IQ is supposed to be a secret, but secrets have ways of being told, and told they were. If parents found out that their child had a high IQ little time was lost in spreading the good news. If the IQ was 100 or so there was often resentment toward teachers, school, and other parents who could afford to boast.

All this was not lost on the children concerned! If they were bright they might lord it over others or secretly think of themselves as something special.

Then there was the truly intelligent parent who challenged the school. "You have tested these children and some of them are superior material. *What are you planning to do now?"*

A very good question! Let's investigate briefly some of the plans made for the enriched curriculum of high IQ children, plans made with the hope of training these bright minds to better use their gifts.

HOMOGENEOUS GROUPING

Probably the oldest and most familiar method of trying to do the best for the bright child, and for the slow child too, is separating them from each other. This seemed to be the answer. But here again the Great Majority enters the picture. Suppose you were a principal planning your organization. You would take the brightest children in the grade and put them in one class, and take the slowest in the grade and put *them* in one class—and where would you be then? No teacher of a medium group is going to stand for it if he has 40 children to deal with and the other teachers on the grade have only a handful. The next best thing would be to slip the top of your medium group into the bright group and the bottom of it into the slow group, and there you are, very much in the same position you were before you started!

Then some person who has a large voice in the operation of your school system complains, "This is not a real life situation. These children will have to meet and live with all levels of intelligence when they face the world. The only sensible way for children to be educated is in a heterogeneous group." And if the voice is loud enough and has enough influence back we all go to the old method. Back and forth and back again every few years. The pendulum swings and the teacher must swing with it.

THE IGC EXPERIMENT

Here and there larger school systems tried to meet the problem of training intellectually gifted children by forming classes for them in central locations and busing them in from other schools. Teachers were selected, many of them specially trained to work with bright children. The classes went under several names to protect the youngsters in them from the "stigma" of being considered smarter than the run-of-the-mill. The "IG" or the "IGC" were labels often attached to them and everyone was a bit reluctant to say just what the letters meant.

It wasn't long before parents of other children began asking questions and demanding answers. "If it's a question of superior intelligence," they said, "some sad mistakes are being made." Unwilling tots were dragged to psychologists to be tested so that they too might joint the elite (so called "stigma" notwithstanding). The atmosphere was so often not conducive to the good of *any* of the children in the school that one class after another was dissolved, and the poor little guinea pigs returned to their neighborhood schools.

AND WHAT OF RAPID ADVANCEMENT?

Through the years bright children were often skipped. Most of them survived the experience, but after a skip or two a child would find himself in high school surrounded by giants who wanted nothing to do with them.

"Well then," sighed the educators, "let's put these bright youngsters into classes that will advance more rapidly. Let them do three years' work in two. They'll be together and will be a challenge to each other. They'll study an enriched curriculum, and with smaller classes such as these the teachers can observe their special abilities and give them the necessary guidance."

A good, sound idea and sometimes it works beautifully—in the type of community where parents have the best interests of their children at heart. But in a status-centered setup, in a community where it is a reflection on parents *not* to have their child in such a group, the child becomes a vehicle for his parents' vanity. Ask any teacher in a suburb with a "good post office address" and he can tell you one story after another, stories that would make you ill, of the nervous little wrecks who are being used by their parents to impress the neighbors with the superiority of the family.

THERE IS NEVER COMPLETE AGREEMENT ABOUT THE HANDLING OF BRIGHT CHILDREN

There has been bitter disagreement about the handling of bright children. There have been unfortunate errors in judgment. Educators mean well, but the perfect formula is still to be found. In spite of this many of our gifted children prove themselves as they mature. Some have been rescued from mediocrity by the sympathetic understanding of a classroom teacher who saw in them some talent or gift and provided opportunities for its expression.

WHAT ABOUT YOUR OWN CLASS?

Now, take your own case. You have what is commonly known as a heterogeneous group (you're in that swing of the pendulum). You are familiar with the achievement record of each child in your class. Reading achievement, considered one of the important signs of intelligence, varies as much as three years, while the difference in age is 11 months.

In the group that you secretly call your bright ones there are five children. They're using a basic reader and workbook two years in advance of the grade, and they've read everything you have on the library shelves. Let's have a closer look at these youngsters. Suppose we begin with the twins. "Smart as a whip," their teachers say.

1. Evelyn and Bill are very close but are as different as day and night. Both rate high in achievement in math and reading. Evelyn is practical, Bill is a dreamer. When Evelyn finishes an assignment she quietly goes to her "class" as she calls them, a group of three she's adopted and to whom she gives a great deal of voluntary help. She checks with each one to see if he needs any assistance. Once satisfied that they're doing all right, Evelyn tiptoes to the supply closet, for the teacher has asked her to keep an eye on what materials need to be ordered on the next supply date. While there she straightens out the stacks of paper and does a bit of dusting. The class is still busy with the assignment so Evelyn goes to the encyclopedia to find some more facts on the history of stringed instruments.

2. Bill finishes his assignment as quickly as his twin. He looks around the room in a leisurely manner, takes out a pad, and begins to sketch his sister. This reminds him that he promised to complete the first section of a mural of ancient instruments and he strolls to the back of the room with his drawing pencil.

3. Mary is a bright child too, bright in the know-it-all way common to spoiled children. Her work is done quickly, but it's careless and sloppy looking. When you tell her to change, correct, or re-do a paper she's resentful and often resorts to tears. She doesn't have the inner resources of the

twins, never has any plan of what she'll do next, and is a prime time-waster and a nuisance to those sitting near her.

4. Bob is a big, overgrown child, clumsy in the manner of those who can't seem to catch up with their rapid growth. He insists on running in the hall, loves to read, and is affectionate but touchy. A real history buff and a lover of facts, he's the terror of the child who's poorly prepared for a report. Bob would love to be a baseball champ but he's never yet caught a fly ball. He's interested in everything and would like to have a finger in everybody's pie.

5. Reggie is a real pepper pot who's ready to fight at the mere suggestion of amusement at his name. He's a whiz at math and reading presents no problem, but his first love is astronomy. The youngest of four brothers, all bright, he often uses words his classmates have never heard. The parents are well educated and encourage the boys to join in family discussions of far out subjects. Reggie's biggest problem is adjusting to the seeming simplicity of classroom procedure.

CAN ONE TEACHER TAKE CARE OF THIS BRIGHT GROUP?

Which of these children needs help? Which of them would profit most by being moved to a different class, if such a thing is possible in your school?

The twins are happy. They like you and their class, and like being together. Each is doing good work and contributing to the smooth functioning of the group. Each is able to improve the time not needed for actual lessons. Evelyn has the makings of a good secretary or perhaps a teacher. She has often told you that she wants to be one or the other. Bill may become a professor, or perhaps an artist, or combine the two for a full, interesting life. The family is musical, reads together, and is a happy, close-knit unit. Lucky children!

Mary's type is known to all teachers. She needs guidance and you have reason to believe she's not getting it at home. Well, if she needs it and isn't getting it, it's up to you. Tackle the time-wasting first. Help her make a list of ideas for using her extra time wisely and interestingly. She'll like that for it will help to make her feel important, something she needs greatly. You might team her up with Evelyn if you think it wise. The more stable child could have a fine influence upon her. You may find that her careless manner and attitude toward life in general improve as her self-confidence is strengthened.

Bob's doing all right. Be as patient as you can with his running and clumsiness. Tell him confidentially that you understand how he feels about people who don't have his deep respect for facts of all kinds. His baseball skills will improve as he catches up with himself physically. There's no real problem here. Bob likes you and the class. His interests are wide. He's working up to his ability.

But what about this Reggie? Unquestionably it is *he* who would profit most from a change of environment. Inquire about the possibility of placing him in a class where the general level of intelligence is high. In the meantime let him take on a special assignment in science. Perhaps he and a kindred spirit in a neighboring class can work out a series of simple lectures on the heavenly bodies. Then they can offer to present these lectures to other classes. Or they might show a filmstrip of their own making on the constellations, taking care of the running comment and asking and answering questions. Suppose these two teammates start a science club. Reggie will go along with you, for he's looking desperately for some way to occupy that busy brain.

USE WHAT A BRIGHT CHILD HAS TO OFFER

What strong points do your bright children have? Is it an unusual ability and interest in science? In music? In art? Does one of them have the knack of helping slower classmates with their research, or math, or perhaps even penmanship? Take each child's strong point and help him use it so that he *and* the class profit from this special ability.

Insist that your bright children: (1) complete their own assignments, (2) help in classroom management, (3) *assist others.* Then you may encourage the poet in one, or the musician in another, the mathematician or the budding scientist, by giving them the *privilege* of contributing this special ability to the enrichment of the entire group. Your guidance is necessary. Sometimes just a suggestion from you at the right time is all that such a child needs to start a new project rolling. If he has a plan of his own listen to it, and if it has any merit encourage him to carry it out. You can give him the necessary help as the need may arise.

You *can* keep your bright children busy, happy, and helpful. They *can* have an enriched curriculum in your heterogeneous class. Don't permit them to waste their gifts by doing boring, repetitious assignments when they have so much to offer. *And don't countenance lazy performance from them!*

WHAT TO DO ABOUT ELLEN!

Ellen's case is more unusual. Not only is she bright but she is gifted musically. At the age of seven she played the piano so well she appeared in concerts. Whether it was Bach or Chopin she seemed to understand what the composer was trying to say and interpreted the music in a sympathetic manner.

Now, at 11, she is high-strung, doing everything in a quick, nervous way. Her schoolwork presents no problem for she treats her studies in the same competent manner she tackles music lessons. There is an impatience about the child although she is never rude. To quote her teacher, "Ellen acts in the classroom as though she were a polite adult mistakenly thrown in with a group of children and trying to make the best of it."

But this teacher realized that Ellen needed something more than the environment of her own classroom could offer. In another year she would be accepted at a special school for gifted youngsters, but what could be done for her now? As so often happens the answer came from an unexpected quarter.

Ellen is the monitor for the second grade. She calls for "her" children in the playground, brings them upstairs, and helps the teacher get them started. At 9 AM she is expected to be in her own classroom. She loves the little ones and treats them as though she were their big, understanding sister. One morning Ellen came into her own classroom an hour late, face shining, completely oblivious of the fact that her teacher had not known where she was.

"Mr. Preston," she exclaimed, "I've been having a wonderful time! Miss Leonard's car broke down and she just arrived. And what do you think I've been doing? Talking about Brahms and teaching his *Lullaby* to the second graders! And they loved it! And Miss Leonard wants to know if I can help her with the singing and music appreciation lessons!"

Mr. Preston realized that this could be the answer for Ellen. Of course there would be the formality of securing permission from the principal, but that shouldn't be difficult. What an opportunity for this gifted child to fill a personal need and serve her school at the same time!

THE CURRICULUM IS PLANNED FOR THE MAJORITY OF THE CHILDREN

The great majority of the children in our schools falls somewhere into place between the two extremes of the very bright and the very slow. A curriculum is planned with this majority in mind. The bright child can become bored without a real challenge. The slow child may gradually abandon the struggle to keep up with his class. You are doing the best you can for the group as a whole and these two extremes of ability present added problems. You must challenge the bright group and enrich their curriculum while you pull the slow group along with the most elementary kind of work. You're helping Reggie plan a science experiment while your slow pupils struggle with phonics. And all the while there's the great middle group demanding most of your attention.

THE SLOW CHILD IN THE CLASSROOM SETUP

The slow child, even when he can read orally, is usually slow to comprehend the content of what he's reading. I remember one girl of 11 who read aloud like an angel, had the voice of an angel, and never understood one word of what she read. This child couldn't do the simplest problem in math, nor could she find the United States on a map of North America after months of work on the subject. But read aloud? No trouble.

More often the slow child has difficulty with any form of reading. The phonics he conquers today must be tackled again tomorrow. The sentence or two so painfully written must be started all over again next time. The saddest part of this is that failure seems to breed failure, and after a series of such experiences the child expects nothing else and hope departs. Then we find ourselves with a child who has locked himself in a little world of his own making, where he has to compete with no one and can dream his own dreams. Or, as frequently happens, he gets the satisfaction and attention he craves by becoming the devil incarnate.

Is there any way in which a child of little ability can be permitted to feel that there is something *he* can do very well, perhaps better than others?

Ten year old Jeanette used a second grade workbook. After a reading period with her teacher and two children using the same level book, this group would be assigned a page of follow-up work to be done while the teacher tackled the rest of her class. Inevitably Jeanette would wander to the back of the room and start cleaning the sink. When her teacher rebuked her for neglecting the workbook Jeanette would always say, "I can't stand a dirty sink, Miss Simon. Doesn't it look better now?"

On one memorable day Miss Simon had an inspiration. She printed on a sheet of paper—

Dear Jeanette,

The sink is shining and clean. Thank you.

Miss Simon

Then she watched for the child's reaction. After a moment or two a small smile appeared. She turned to her teacher and said, "I know this is my name, Jeanette." Miss Simon nodded. "Is this word sink?" Again Miss Simon nodded. "And is this word sh–shi–shine?" (Her first attempts to use phonics of her own free will.)

Such a small success! "Read it all to me, Miss Simon." And Miss Simon did. The girl read it again and again. She pasted it in her notebook and took it home for Mother to see. The next morning she smiled shyly at her teacher and proceeded to the sink where she taped a sign which read—

I SHINE THE SINK

JEANETTE

That day she wrote three short sentences and asked her teacher to please "fix them right."

If failure breeds failure the opposite is also true. Success encourages success. Jeanette was no overnight sensation, but that wall of failure and discouragement had cracked. The child's reading and attempts at composition were sink-centered for some days. Then her teacher (who was learning something, too) broadened the horizon to include the paint pots and brushes, and these became a new subject of interest. Gradually the child lost her fear of attempting to read and write.

WHEN A SLOW CHILD FOLLOWS A BRIGHT SIBLING

Eddie's experience was different from Jeanette's. In the classroom he was shy, slow in all his work, but always smiling and courteous. He was three years younger than a very bright sister, the kind of child who has no difficulty with schoolwork and can do nearly everything perfectly. His mother, a charming little lady who shared her good looks with her son, confided to me that Eddie had suffered since first grade from the fact that his sister, Corinne, was such an able student. "If only people would refrain from comparing the two children," she said despairingly, "Eddie might have half a chance. I can't believe he's truly dull!"

I agreed completely with the mother. Eddie was definitely not dull. To watch him on the athletic field was a joy. He moved swiftly and gracefully. He was the picture of self-confidence in any game, and was always the unanimous choice for captain of the team. It is interesting to note that athletics was the one exception to Corinne's record of perfection. In games she was slow and awkward, and consequently uninterested.

"Here is the answer," thought I smugly. "I'll use this interest in athletics as a starting point and I'll have him reading and doing some math in a month."

I came up against a blank wall of resistance. Athletics on the field? Yes. In the classroom? Eddie tightened up as though he thought I was trying to trick him. The breakthrough came in a way neither of us had ever expected.

In the late winter I brought some apple branches into the classroom. Children enjoy watching such things as forsythia bloom indoors, but this was the first time I had experimented with apple branches. We talked about them, what they would need, when we might expect some blossoms, etc. Eddie listened courteously, he always did that, but took no part in the discussion. We placed the bare, brown branches in a bowl of water on the science table where they remained, looking very dead. Forsythia branches bloomed and faded, the apple branches seemed to do nothing.

Every morning Eddie would go to the science table as soon as he came into the room. He would take the magnifying glass and study our seemingly hopeless experiment, turn away and take his seat. I was pleased that he took such an interest, but I wasn't smart enough to put two and two together.

There was a cold, wet snow one morning in early spring. Eddie went directly to the apple branches without removing coat or boots. He took the magnifying glass as usual, studied his pet subject for a moment, turned around, and yelled! Our courteous, quiet Eddie yelled! "They're blooming! The apples are blooming!" After an instant of stunned silence we crowded around him. His good manners returned and he offered me the magnifying glass first. Sure enough! A tiny bit of delicate pink showed under the glass.

"Eddie," I said, "you've done it! You were the first to discover our blooms. You never gave up hope."

The boy flushed with pride and smilingly took charge while his classmates took turns to have Eddie show them the wonder of nature that he had discovered. I talked with him when things quieted down and found out that he had a natural green thumb. He planted and cultivated the family garden and his grandmother's too. He told me that his room at home was crowded with all kinds of experiments with growing things. We had found the opening in the wall! Gardening was his first love—athletics just happened.

Sometimes it seems that we will never find the key to the awakening of a child's interest, and now and then we fail miserably. There are some children who appear dull and lifeless as long as they are in our classes. We try half-heartedly from time to time to break through their resistance to learning. But when success comes it makes up for a great deal.

TOMMY LACKED SELF-CONFIDENCE

Tommy was fat—just plain fat! His mother maintained that it was hereditary, and maybe it was. But she would tell me from time to time of the child's unhappiness and I couldn't help but suspect that his one comfort might be food. It certainly wasn't school, for his performance was poor in most subjects, and to make matters worse he wasn't accepted by the other boys.

But Tommy could sing! He had the sweet flutelike quality of voice that belongs only to the boy soprano, and when he was singing he was transformed from an unhappy little fat boy to a confident person in his own right. I had made more than one attempt to carry over this unconsciousness of self into his studies, but he would have none of it. As soon as we turned to reading or math Tommy froze up and all his fear of failure returned.

One day the boy came to see me and said that his mother thought he should join my glee club. I had asked him several times for the group needed his lovely voice, but he had politely refused. Now he was making a small overture, so I told him how welcome he would be.

He was a fine addition to our singing group and seemed to be enjoying himself at rehearsals. When we started to plan our spring concert Tommy offered some good suggestions about songs we might sing and how we might arrange each number. But when he came back to the classroom he turned into the same timid boy again.

I thought a word or two whispered in the right ears might help so I asked the president of our glee club (a big, capable girl) if she thought we could get Tommy to sing a solo, or at least a solo part. She was enthusiastic and started a sort of whispering campaign to "draft Tommy" for a solo in the spring concert. Even so, I was somewhat surprised when he agreed. He would like to sing "Danny Boy," a perfect selection for his voice, but only if he could sing from behind the stage curtain.

"All right," said I. "Let's begin to rehearse."

He and I practiced before school, during lunch hours, after school. Tommy came out from behind the curtain and sang, and finally came down to stand beside the piano and sang. It was beautiful and he knew it. He sang "Danny Boy" for the glee club and the members applauded and praised him.

When the day of the concert arrived Tommy was in fine voice and only moderately excited. He took his place by the piano. The first few notes seemed a bit low for him and I wondered if he would make it. Then he took a deep breath and really started to sing.

The last sweet notes died away and then the applause started. Tommy smiled and bowed like a seasoned operatic tenor. Finally the principal came beaming down the aisle and held up his hand for silence. He thanked Tommy and told him how proud he and the children were of his fine performance. The boy responded graciously as though he did such things every day of the week.

After the concert Tommy's mother came to see me, her eyes brimming with tears.

"This has been so wonderful for Tommy," she said. "He's entirely different at home and his father and I can scarcely believe it. Has his schoolwork improved? Do you think it will?"

Tommy never set any records scholastically but he no longer was afraid to try. He left the slow reading group behind and advanced to the second group. The most important thing of all was that he had earned the respect and admiration of others and now had the confidence in himself that had been so lacking.

TRY TO FIND THE CHILD'S "LONG SUIT"

A bright child may seem lazy because he's bored with school. He has ability but not the opportunity to use it. *Find the time* to talk with him about his interests and hopes. Give him the *privilege* of sharing these interests with others. Once he has the experience of a challenging activity he can offer a great deal to his classmates.

And this child who is considered slow or even dull. He may be just that, and still have the makings of a good, substantial member of society. Let's not put him on the hopeless list. No one but Edison's mother had any faith in him; he was considered cloddish by his teacher. Nor was Einstein a miracle child. Some children are slow starters, but when they get their teeth into something that appeals to them, when they *do* start, things happen!

—— HELPING THE TOP AND BOTTOM OF —— YOUR CLASS

The curriculum is prepared for the great majority of our children. Those who are exceptionally bright and those who cannot keep up present added problems to the teacher.

A bright child must be handled wisely, given an opportunity to use his gifts, or he may become bored with school. He may possibly develop into a disciplinary problem or simply withdraw.

Some time ago much emphasis was placed upon intelligence testing and IQ scores, but we have come to realize that it is not necessarily a true picture of a child's ability.

Several types of homogeneous grouping have been tried such as special classes for the gifted or rapid advancement of the children.

The bright children in any heterogeneous group vary greatly in their interests and abilities. It is up to the classroom teacher of such a group to help the bright children use their gifts to the greatest advantage to themselves and their classmates.

Encourage your abler pupils to share their interests with others. Insist that they complete their own assignments in a satisfactory way.

A slow child in a heterogeneous group may withdraw because he cannot cope or he can become a disciplinary problem.

To motivate the interest of a slow child find some one thing he can do well. If it is simply the willingness to clean the sink, start with that, for you have to start somewhere.

Such a child usually lacks confidence, and if he can show his classmates that there is something he can do well it's a step in the right direction.

REMEMBER—FAILURE BREEDS FAILURE, BUT FORTUNATELY, SUCCESS ENCOURAGES SUCCESS.

Chapter Ten ～

Discipline: Rules and Rebels

$\mathcal{W}$hen teachers hear the word "discipline" a definite picture comes to mind—keeping order in the classroom, one of our biggest jobs and frequently the most difficult.

There are all kinds of discipline, in the classroom and out of it, and there are all types of disciplinarians. We know teachers who are martinets, and we know teachers who are too easy. We know an occasional teacher who is a bully, and we know teachers who try to be so "understanding" that they are lax in the handling of children.

There *has* to be discipline in life. The discipline that a dancer, or a singer, or a concert pianist forces upon himself is essential to his success. To more ordinary mortals this rigid discipline is unnecessary, but all of us need direction and boundaries. All of us must learn *to inhibit, to keep ourselves in hand, to grow up.*

WHAT OF PERMISSIVENESS?

A child raised in a permissive atmosphere is insecure. Take, for example, one whose parents "love" him too much to refuse him anything. He is asked what he wants to eat, when or if he wants to go to bed, what shirt or tie he prefers to wear. We laugh at the expression, "Decisions! Decisions!" but it's not funny when a child must decide every little detail of his daily existence. He is badly confused and may develop into a nervous wreck or a first rate tyrant, or both, and rule his parents with an iron hand.

Children need direction. They must have someone to guide them, for how can a child judge what is best for himself, what is

153

wise or unwise? There must be an adult who will say "No!" when it's necessary. Someone has said that children need fences. They unconsciously yearn for direction and rules, and to give them this is a responsibility that belongs to parents and teachers. We do a child no favor when we permit him to grow up doing as he pleases.

Does this mean that a child should be constantly thwarted and frustrated in his attempts to discover his own capabilities, refused permission to try *anything* interesting? Of course not! Under intelligent guidance children learn to choose between the acceptable and the unacceptable. They learn that manners are necessary, that consideration for others is a way of life. Such guidance does not crush their spirit, as the permissive advocates seem to fear, but lays the foundation on which true self-expression is built.

WHEN DO WE BEGIN?

Most tots are anxious to go to school. They watch older brothers and sisters coming and going with books under their arms and are impatient for the day when some of the great mysteries will be explained to them. They want to do what others do and can't *wait* to conform.

Teachers of early grades can use this urge to great advantage in training little children to work as members of a group. Years ago the "good" children sat quietly, hands folded, lips tight shut. The "bad" ones talked out at any time, left their seats, ran around the room. Some of our well-meaning teachers of long ago would be shocked to see a capably run classroom of today where small children have opportunities to move from one place to another, find their library books, enter into class discussions, talk freely with teacher.

A gentleman of our acquaintance who was brought up under the old-fashioned method of classroom management tells us that in the first grade he determined that he would become a teacher because his teacher *could walk around the room* while *he* sat with hands folded on the edge of the desk. At that time he could think of nothing more desirable than being able to move around the room at will.

THAT BUGABOO, CONFORMITY

Since our friend attended first grade things have changed. For a time it was the fashion to be permissive—allow too much freedom, too little supervision. The teacher who was forced into this impossible position was at her wit's end. If she used her common sense and tried a middle course she was frequently criticized. The child was King! Discipline was discouraged. There was no firm hand. Marks and morale fell together. Conformity was a bad word.

Then came the shock of finding out that our children with their freedom of choice, our children who were unfettered by conformity, were not the brightest in the world. Other countries who trained their children with a firm hand and insisted on discipline in school—such countries were surpassing us in sports, in technology, in all-round ability. The wrath of people in high places was directed at the schools. Who else could be blamed? There had to be a scapegoat.

"What," they demanded, "are the schools going to do about it?"

DISCIPLINE RETURNS TO THE CLASSROOM

One of the first moves was a general tightening of the reins. Those in high places realized that our children must have direction, there must be someone with the authority to insist on a job well done. The old grim discipline of years back was unacceptable but our students must conform to the old ideals of hard work and good manners. Could we combine the firm hand of the old with the enlightened views of the new? We would try. To the surprise of a good many people *the children like it!* They take pride in a piece of work well done. They are not afraid to admit that Mr. Donaldson or Miss Miles ("Man! Are they strict!") are the best teachers they ever had, and "I never thought I'd like math!" (Or science, or calisthenics.)

Teachers are once again challenging their students and are finding them much more capable of meeting challenges than we had supposed. This doesn't mean that all the fun has gone out of learning. There's still time for the story, for the game that teaches or reviews a lesson. Children are accepting the fact that much of their schoolwork requires concentration, hard digging, and time.

HOW MUCH CONFORMITY IS NECESSARY IN THE CLASSROOM?

In kindergarten and in first grade children have to learn *and* observe certain procedures that are essential to their safety and well-being. (See Chapter Two.) They are trained to work with others, to respond to directions from the teacher, to accept their share of responsibility in caring for the classroom. In short, to cooperate. As we found out in Chapter Two, all this is accomplished very slowly, with much repetition and endless patience. But little tots respond well to such training and the great majority enjoy being working members of a group.

As children advance through the second and third grades most of those who rebelled at the beginning of their school careers have calmed down. Teachers who had difficulty with them in the early years often remark about the change in such children when they see them in the lunchroom or the play yard. They have made the necessary adjustment and have conformed to the most important rules of safety and conduct with no harm to themselves.

THERE'S ALWAYS THE REBEL!

Most active, intelligent people have a touch of the rebel in their makeup. They question the infallibility of the "establishment" and see ways in which it could be improved. Such rebels have accounted for many of the worthwhile advances in history, and we are grateful to them.

It is the rebel without a cause who worries us. He rebels as a way of life; he is angry and recalcitrant. He defies authority for the sake of defiance. How should the teacher deal with the rebel in the classroom?

WHAT IS RECALCITRANCE?

According to the dictionary a recalcitrant person is "not amenable to control, resists authority, is sullenly or perversely obstinate." The same definitions are used interchangeably for one who is "refractory." Teachers who have dealt day in and day out with such children can add a few interesting comments. One refractory child in a class is enough to disturb an entire group. The attention he demands takes the energy and goodwill of the teacher. Time spent on him is lost to his classmates.

How do you deal with recalcitrance?

Here are five types of refractory behavior and the account of the way in which each was handled successfully.

OVER EXUBERANCE

We've all met the child with an overabundance of animal spirits. He can be a cause of trouble in the room and especially in the playground or lunchroom. When you come right down to it he's the easiest problem child to help. Rarely is he nasty or sullen. He fights, he yells, he manages to get others involved in his escapades, but you *can* talk with him and he'll talk with you.

Mrs. Drake had such a child in her fifth grade, a medium bright group of interested boys and girls. They resented Danny because he was responsible for almost daily reports and complaints from the yard and Safety Patrols. The children took great pride in their class and wanted it to look good, and Danny was the one child who drew unfavorable attention to 5–3.

Then, too, Danny was usually late because he would all too willingly become involved in situations on the way to school, situations which his classmates would either avoid or ignore. There was a dog to be seen safely through the traffic, or a fire engine that must be followed, and an occasional wild story about a holdup or a free-for-all.

Even Mrs. Drake, who had the reputation of liking the nonconformists, was getting enough of Danny. With her sense of humor she managed to keep him in line when she was with him, but without her restraining influence anything could happen and frequently did. The child's mother was not much help for she was the breadwinner and away at work all day. His grandmother, who was in charge at home, worshiped him—he could do no wrong. She told Mrs. Drake that Danny was a good boy, always kind and loving—he had just too much pep. His father had been like that and if he were there Danny wouldn't get into scrapes. A boy needs a man around, it's no good with two women—the grandmother went on and on.

Mrs. Drake let her talk. A plan was beginning to form in her mind. If Danny needed a man in his life, perhaps Mr. Fusaro could help. But there were so many boys in *his* life, could he make room for another? At the first opportunity she cornered Mr. Fusaro. He taught a fifth year class too, and had resisted all efforts to go to another grade. This was the place for him because there was something about kids of 10 or 11 which appealed to him, and the children seemed to know it and adored the man. If only Danny had been placed in Mr. Fusaro's class, but it was too late for that!

In addition to his regular duties Mr. Fusaro taught woodworking to the boys of several grades. At home he had an understanding wife and a workshop where some of the neighborhood boys gathered once or twice a week to work on special projects. They had made up their own set of rules for the running of this one man boys' club and each must comply or else!

"Could Danny possibly be admitted to your club?" asked Mrs. Drake.

Mr. Fusaro rubbed his chin thoughtfully. "Actually it's not my club," he answered. "The boys run it under my guidance and any new applicant must prove his sincerity before he's accepted. I know your Danny. He's in one of my woodworking classes. Likeable kid, but on the wild side. I don't know."

"But he needs the companionship of boys and a man," said Mrs. Drake. "He needs someone to make him toe the line. At home there's nobody to make him do *anything*. I can manage him in school, but that's not enough. He needs some rules to live by."

"I'll talk with him next woodworking day," said Mr. Fusaro. "I'll sound him out anyway but no promises yet."

Danny came back from his next woodworking class and announced loudly as he opened the door, "Hey! Mr. Fusaro wants me to bring my bookshelf over to his shop at his house! He's got a special tool there that I can use."

A few days later Danny came as far as his teacher's desk before he announced that he was "on probation" in Mr. Fusaro's club. "Do you think they might let me join? They got awful strict rules, but I wish—I hope I can."

There was one sad day for Danny when the club voted to extend his period of probation rather than admit him to membership. It seems that Mrs. Fusaro, a silent member of the club, but a member with a vote, had insisted that the boy learn to speak in a normal voice instead of yelling. He was temporarily crushed.

"Women!" he growled. "Who needs them!"

Danny joined the club and knuckled down to rules for the first time in his young life. He won the great privilege of putting on the gloves for a round or two in the homemade ring. Eventually he learned to take some real punches without losing his temper.

Boys' clubs, when they're available, have changed many a child's attitude toward law and order. Too few people are willing to devote their leisure to such a cause. The Fusaro's love it but they're rather unusual people.

NO TWO PROBLEMS ARE ALIKE

You can't make neat little boxes and fit children into them. Those who seem to have the same problem often react differently to the same treatment. Parental neglect makes one child in the family a delinquent and a brother or sister a frightened, silent child. Too strict a home produces one child who need reassurance from everyone and another who takes pleasure in rebelling against all the rules in the book.

In your classroom you will find a problem child who responds well to a firm hand or just a good bawling out, while another goes from bad to worse with the same handling. There can be no hard and fast rules; you are the one who must study and experiment. Use your judgment, your common sense, your experience. Consult available records, talk with the school nurse (who has probably visited the home), talk with the parent (at least give it a try). By all means talk with your supervisor whose experience is of necessity wider than your own. If the nurse or supervisor thinks it wise to refer the case to a staff psychologist, that may prove to be the solution to the problem.

WHEN THE CHILD WITHDRAWS

Take Ronald, for example. He was no trouble to his teacher; he sat all day and drew maps (once you had furnished him with his daily pencil). That was *it;* he drew maps. He didn't talk to you, nor did he answer you. He drew maps, and smiled occasionally. After the third visit to the psychologist that good man said to him, "There's no need for you to come again, Ronnie. You're OK. But I'm making an appointment for your mother, and she'd better keep it!" (And the boy reported this to his teacher of his own free will.)

It seems that Ronnie's mother, although earnest and devoted to her family, was a compulsive talker; she just couldn't shut up!

The child had built a neat little wall of silence to keep her out. On the other hand, the sister, two years younger, was a bright, able student who seemed unaffected by her mother's double-hinged tongue. Some personalities mesh gears well, some can ignore each other, and some are pure poison when they come in contact. How disastrous this can be when the personalities involved are parent and child!

SOME CHILDREN ARE MEAN!

When Jack was an infant his family was forced to leave their European home for political reasons. They settled temporarily in South America, then in the Caribbean Islands, and finally in the United States. At the time of their arrival here Jack was 10 and as mean as they come. His eight-year-old brother was calm and easy-going, but very much afraid of Jack, who abused him at every opportunity. The boy didn't look mean—in fact, he was rather attractive with a round face and blond hair, and he had us all fooled for a short time.

Then the complaints began to pile up. An irate parent came to see the principal about Jack. He had stabbed her child, who happened to be in front of him on line, with a sharp pencil and had given warning that he'd better not tell the teacher. He tossed a classmate's books into a mud puddle. He turned over a bottle of ink on another child's prized drawing. His ingenuity was amazing.

It was hard to believe the reports for I had never caught him in any one of these acts. Could there be a conspiracy against the newcomer? Could these children be ganging up on Jack?

I talked with the boy and he categorically denied all charges. I talked with the complainants and found their stories very convincing, but Jack made his denial convincing too. I talked with the mother, and the only "satisfaction" was her request that I should see that he took his medicine at a certain time each morning.

Something had to be done, for at the rate he was going Jack was bound to do some real damage at any moment. I told the boy frankly that I would keep my eagle eye on him and find out the truth for myself. We would have another talk soon.

During the next few days I compiled the following list of offenses seen with my own eyes:

1. He decorated a white shirt ahead of him on line with fountain-pen ink.
2. He asked to leave the line going to assembly because he had forgotten his handkerchief. I followed him and found that he was pulling our hand-raised seedlings out of their pots and leaving them on the windowsill to die.
3. He stuck out his foot during a race in gym period and sent a child flying.
4. He removed a cherished, elaborately decorated book report from the bulletin board and calmly put it in the wastebasket.
5. He put a dirty rubber on his neighbor's lunch when the child looked away for a moment at the lunch table.

Then I faced Jack with the list. He neither affirmed nor denied any of the evidence. He simply stuck out his jaw and stared at me.

"Jack," I said, "none of us is happy about this situation. The children are learning to distrust and dislike you. You must know how your teacher feels about it. And I'm very, very sure you're not happy either."

Up until that moment I hadn't the faintest idea of what to do. He probably needed a good shellacking but, unfortunately, that was outside my province. I told him in words of one syllable that he would have *one week* to improve his relations with his class-mates. The mean tricks would have to stop. He *must* begin to act like a decent citizen. We would help, but the first steps were up to him.

There was the merest hint of a smile on his face, the first I had ever seen from him, and to tell the truth I didn't know whether that boded good or bad.

"I'd like to try *not* punching people around on line," he said, "but only for a week." Then he added, "But I want the kids to know I'm trying."

I had thought this would be a secret between him and me, but if Jack wanted it publicized, all right. We informed the class and they were interested and very serious about the arrangement. I told the boy I wanted a daily check to see if he too was serious about it. He agreed.

The children in the class were really wonderful—and after all they had suffered at his hands! They cooperated by not creating any situation that might cause Jack to forget his promise. He discovered that when he refrained from punching on line it was easier to refrain from other mean tricks, and he was touchingly proud when at the end of the first week, his punching record was clean. The following week he made more acceptable behavior in the lunchroom his goal with moderate success. His classmates followed Jack's gradual conversion with all the interest of soap opera devotees.

One week he decided not to beat up his little brother and brought the child to me to confirm the miracle. It was not always a perfect record. Being human he fell from grace once in a while, but he was becoming a more acceptable member of society.

When Jack was promoted to the sixth grade he went to a teacher who was fair and *strict*. I checked now and then to see how things were working out, but there was no unusual complaint.

WHEN THE PSYCHOLOGIST'S HELP IS NEEDED

Wally came to us the day our beautiful new school opened. He had been transferred from an overcrowded building nearby, but we were unaware of the rejoicing going on there now that they were rid of him.

The boy was immaculately dressed, every hair in place, shoes shined—and a perfect devil. The first few days were comparatively uneventful as teacher, class, and Wally too, were busy getting acquainted with an entirely new setup.

Along came the first fire drill with everyone concentrating on finding the right exit and the right place to stand outside. Wally tore past his teacher, out the door like a cyclone, and through the kindergarten line, scattering screaming tots like chaff. It was a complete disaster!

In the inevitable conference that followed with the principal, Wally's teacher found out that the boy's record from kindergarten to fifth grade showed very poor work and something else that was variously described by the comments of a succession of teachers as being all the way from "emotionally unstable" to plain "crazy."

You might ask, "Shouldn't the teacher have previewed the class records before she met the children—studied confidential reports of previous teachers, etc? Isn't that the best way to avoid such unpleasant surprises?" But in this case the records were unavoidably late in arriving from the three "feeding schools" as our building was unfinished until mid-August.

Since it was too late for that, what could be done now? When the records arrived they showed that Wally had been under observation in the district guidance clinic for two years. We were informed that the psychologist who handled this case would visit soon and have a conference with teacher and principal. In fact, although there was a long waiting list on his agenda, he was coming that Friday. Would we please have a written record of everything connected with Wally that had transpired since opening day?

The psychologist met with the principal and Wally's teacher and was deadly serious about the boy.

"I beg you," he said, "to make every effort to help Wally over this period of adjustment to his new surroundings. I tried to have him kept in the old, familiar school, but since he lives in your district he was sent here. Please believe me when I tell you that he's on the brink of a complete mental breakdown. Help me to keep him from that!"

What could we do but agree to help, but how do you help a child in that precarious state? The rest of the class deserved some consideration from their teacher, too. Would there be time and energy for them?

WAS THERE ANYTHING WALLY COULD DO WELL?

When Wally was in one of his more relaxed moods his teacher talked with him. She discovered that the boy was devoted to horses. He rode well and could talk to and quiet down any horse in the neighboring riding academy, a place he haunted. He dreamed of having a stable of his own someday. As he talked the teacher noticed that his hands kept in motion, almost in time to his speech.

A thought came to her. She would give him an opportunity to lead the class in a choral speaking number—but would he accept the challenge? They were studying Hunt's "Abou Ben Adhem." Wally could never learn those words!

"If Abou Ben Adhem was an Arab and lived on the desert he must have had an Arabian steed," said Wally. He learned the words with little difficulty and led the class so well that the children asked if they might present the number in one of the assembly periods. They did, and it was a great success. Wally led them with all the assurance of a Bernstein.

For a time this was Wally's sole contribution to the class. He would, however, listen to a child's report if it was well done. One day he came to his teacher and announced that he wanted to give a report too about horses. Fine! Did he want someone to help him with research? No, well, maybe to find something about the history of horses, but that would be all.

Ten days later Wally announced that he was ready so we gave him a time allotment in our daily program. He came to the front of the room with six or eight books containing pictures of various breeds of horses and some famous steeds in history.

"Before I start my report on horses," said Wally, "I'm going to ask you to observe a moment of silence in respect for the horse who is such a good friend but who is sometimes treated so badly."

There was an instant of surprise when the children heard this unusual request. Would they laugh? Would everything be ruined? But the children bowed their heads as Wally was doing. There wasn't a smile on any face, just a moving of the eyes as they looked to see how their neighbors were taking it.

"Allah be praised!" breathed the teacher.

Our reporter spoke for 20 minutes to a fascinated audience, and when he finished and asked if there were any questions he answered all that the class put to him, as long as they stayed with the subject of horses.

Here was something that the child loved and could do, and teacher, principal, and psychologist all felt that he had been kept from the threatened "brink." In the next few weeks he led the class in singing and never missed a beat, nor did he ever get silly or temperamental while so engaged.

AREN'T GIRLS EVER DISCIPLINARY PROBLEMS?

There's a sort of legend going round that little girls in the elementary grades are very anxious to please. They love to come up early with the teacher, fuss around the classroom, rearrange shelves and desk drawers, sharpen pencils. They giggle, gossip, cry when things go wrong, usually do their homework, and play school in the afternoon.

Much of this has some truth in it, but both teachers and parents know that little girls—and little boys too—can be perfectly fine at times and perfectly horrible at other times, and we expect that. I know teachers who maintain that when a girl *does* become a behavior problem she is harder to reach. As one veteran puts it, "You can talk to the boys, kid them a bit, rough up their hair. But it's hard to approach a problem girl." This could be an exaggeration, but there is some truth in it.

WE COULDN'T DO ANYTHING WITH BRENDA

From the kindergarten up Brenda had done exactly as she pleased in school, which was exactly nothing constructive. She behaved so badly in the first two years that her overworked teachers were glad to pass her on to the next grade. Her mother said she couldn't help us. She was a mousy little woman with a huge family of boys. She admitted she had given up trying to do anything with the girl and had no time for her.

What did Brenda do in school? In the first place she was always there—no absence for her! She *leered* at the other children, frightening them half to death; leered at her teachers; walked, ran, or crawled around the room at will; opened and shut windows; sang to herself. Her schoolwork was as poor as her behavior. She read after a fashion but only when in the mood, and spelling was the one lesson to which she gave any attention. Then there was the sewing. On rare occasions Brenda would sit quietly with her needle and thread, working away at some little piece of material. Attempts had been made to interest the child in some constructive sewing project, but she had reacted unpleasantly to these. So when Brenda sat quietly, for any reason, no one pushed his luck by interrupting her.

There was one short session with the school psychologist who said nothing was wrong with her. After that all of us seemed to give up trying to do anything about it; we must have felt that everything had been tried at one time or another. I guess we just accepted Brenda as some punishment from the gods—until Mr. Buckly came on the scene.

MR. BUCKLY'S NEW APPROACH

Mr. Buckly came to our school one fall as a complete stranger and fell heir to Brenda. The first day of the school year was no different from any other to her, so she started crawling under desks in the new classroom as she had in the old, familiar one. The teacher saw what was going on and walked over to this strange child.

"Get up off that floor!" he said sternly.

Brenda stood up.

"Go to your seat!" he commanded.

Brenda went.

That was it. Mr. Buckly never had trouble with the girl from that time on. Finding her slow in her studies he helped her, but insisted that she attend to business—and she did.

The rest of the staff asked him about his success with this strange, problem child, but he insisted he had done nothing that he wouldn't do to anyone who was out of order. What was the magic formula? Was it the teacher alone? Could Brenda have been ripe for a personality change? Was there something about this new teacher that clicked in her funny little offbeat mind? Could she have been waiting for some strong person to tell her what to do and no nonsense about it?

This is an example of how firmness is the obvious way to treat such a problem. Sometimes we try everything else, but firmness shown by the right person at the right time is the only answer.

THE "STRONG" TEACHER

Emerson says that it's as easy for the strong to be strong as it is for the weak to be weak. Some teachers can handle a difficult problem with little trouble and others take years to learn. A child may drive one teacher half out of her mind and work beautifully for another. It may be the chemical reaction of personalities, but it is more likely the aura of strength that surrounds some individuals. Children have an uncanny ability to recognize strength or weakness in the adults in their lives.

HOW TO BECOME A "STRONG" TEACHER

There are some basic rules one must follow to become a tower of strength to his pupils. There are techniques learned from experience, some of it bitter, that can be used in general, everyday classroom discipline, techniques that will generously reward you for the effort you must make. Without such rules and techniques one can fumble along year after year, dissatisfied with the profession and resenting any child who doesn't follow the approved pattern of behavior.

RULE #1

Have a well-defined plan: In the first part of this book we explored the necessity of

1. starting off on the right foot the very first day
2. teaching the basic routines and organizing your class-work and pupils
3. planning your work

The "pause that loses attention" *is fatal to your success in dealing with children.* When the attention is permitted to wander, mischief fills the breach. If you are well prepared you have allowed for some flexibility of plan and can keep your composure and your control without a preliminary panic which children with their almost extrasensory perception can spot immediately.

RULE #2

Neither notice everything nor ignore everything: Don't feel that you must point out *all little* infractions of the accepted rules. (I said "little" infractions!) If children feel that their teacher is on their backs every moment and if this teacher makes everything a big deal there can be two unfortunate results: (1) you will find your pupils resenting you and devising ways of flaunting accepted class procedures to spite you, or (2) they'll go underground and become first-rate sneaks. Some tiny infractions are better unnoticed. Your trained eye sees all—but must you *always* impress the children with this remarkable ability? Then, too, you can let a child know he's slightly out of line by a quick look, or even a quizzical half smile. He'll get the picture, and like you better for it. "My teacher's strict but she's a good sport," is high praise from a 10-year-old.

On the other hand, if an incident occurs, an incident you consider important, deal with it at once. DON'T BACK AWAY— DON'T HESITATE! You are responsible for what goes on in the classroom and for your children in and around the building. It is better to treat it at once and make an occasional error in judgment than to make a practice of waiting for a more opportune time. When children know they've misbehaved, as individuals or as a group, they're not going to feel better until someone in authority has punished them.

Two exceptions: There are two exceptions to dealing on the spot with unfortunate incidents. These are occasions when (1) you have reason to believe a child is lying to you, or (2) something has been stolen. In nine cases out of 10 the child will lie when he's accused, for it's the natural thing for a human being to do. Try to prevent this from happening because it's embarrassing to all concerned and sometimes assumes tremendous proportions.

Either of these problems must be handled by you. They cannot be ignored. But *never* approach the solution in public for it is unfair and unwise. It is between you and the child and must be solved by quiet, unhysterical communication between the two of you.

RULE #3

Use—or develop—your sense of humor: Children love a joke! It relieves tension, rests tired nerves, and establishes good rapport between you and them. It can be pure corn, but children love a corny joke or a corny conundrum, and if the joke is too subtle it's lost on them.

Sarcasm is not humor. Using sarcasm on a captive audience of children is cruel and a teacher who descends to this should be corrected. It's even more cruel when it's directed at one child, who has no way of defending himself, than it is when used on the class as a whole. No matter how much you are tempted, never stoop to that level.

Be sure you know your group and your own ability to control it before indulging in humor, even as a tension reliever. Children can get silly at the drop of a hat—they have little sense of the fitness of things—and you'll have your hands full. Feel them out a little at a time and use your judgment. One of our teachers tells her class that a proof of intelligence is the ability to enjoy a good joke and know when to stop laughing.

RULE #4

Never break a promise! Whatever you promise your class, good or bad, see it through. We have discussed this in an earlier chapter but its importance cannot be minimized in maintaining discipline. It bears repetition.

Be wary of threats. When you're tired and the children are demons it's hard to keep the proper perspective. Threats come easily, but you can make a great deal of trouble for yourself if you fall into this trap. Take a deep breath and be *strong!*

If you promise children a game period, a party, a trip, be sure you come through with it. But never *bribe* them with such a promise for that's the weak person's way.

If it's a punishment you've promised, and wish you hadn't, they'll have more respect for the teacher who goes through with it than one who reneges.

RULE #5

Ask for the help of a specialist when necessary: Does this sound like a paradox? Not if you have enough confidence in your own strength to admit that once in a while the opinion or advice of another is needed. You won't make a practice of running here and there for advice, but there are times when even the strong need help. A supervisor who has a hardworking teacher come to him for advice will not consider it weakness on your part. He will do all he can to help you, or perhaps even he too will seek the guidance of a specialist in the kind of problem that has you disturbed.

RULE #6

Do what is necessary to avoid "situations": If you are aware that certain combinations of circumstances upset a problem child and are like a red flag to a bull, it is simple common sense to do what you can to avoid such occurrences. It is not weakness! There is no more reason to allow trouble to start with a difficult child *when it can be avoided with a bit of forethought* than there would be in knocking your head against a stone wall when you could walk around it.

This does not mean tiptoeing around the room trying not to do anything that might cause an unwelcome reaction. It *does* mean that a teacher who is aware, knows his way, has definite aims, and confidence in his own ability develops a sense of timing that is invaluable in handling children even if some of them are problems.

DIFFICULT CLASSES AND DIFFICULT INDIVIDUALS

When dealing with problem children a teacher must be wise, patient, and strong. A child who has trouble adjusting to his surroundings cannot be helped by an upset, hysterical adult. Our job is to do the best we can to mold him into a more acceptable member of society. Each case needs thought, planning, experimenting. We try to give the child the guidance he probably has never received.

The techniques of class discipline were discussed in detail in Chapter Seven. Here we had a teacher faced with the necessity of training an entire class that had gotten out of hand after a year of neglect. Difficult classes and difficult individuals are hard assignments but both must be faced squarely. Both require planning, tact, and endless patience. Of course it is easier for some teachers than it is for others. It is not a question merely of intelligence, for the most important ingredients of successful discipline are personality, moderately good humor, kindness, and *strength*.

─── IS GOOD DISCIPLINE YOUR BIGGEST ─── PROBLEM?

The rigid discipline of the professional performer is not necessary for most of us, but we do need direction and boundaries.

A permissive atmosphere is unhealthy for children both at home and at school. Children need the guiding hand of a wise adult to make them feel secure.

The modern teacher tries to combine the best of the old type of discipline with the more enlightened views of the new.

Most little children starting school *want* to conform. Teachers of early grades can use this to good advantage when training their pupils to observe basic rules of safety and conduct.

Some rebellion is a healthy sign. However, downright recalcitrance must be dealt with firmly, but wisely, for the sake of the individual, the teacher, and the class.

Overexuberance must have some rules, guidance, and an outlet.

The *withdrawn* child needs help. First find the cause of th withdrawal.

A *mean* child has to be taught about the rights of others. He has to be shown the path of decent citizenship in the human race.

If you believe that a psychologist's help is needed consult your supervisor about such a child. It may not be wise to try to deal with it yourself.

There are times when all a problem child needs is a strong teacher to tell him what to do—and fast! But the teacher must have strength and confidence to succeed in this.

Observing basic rules and techniques will help a teacher to become a strong individual able to cope wisely with problems.

Chapter Eleven

Your Professional Relationships
With Other Adults

A good teacher is concerned primarily with the children for whom he is responsible. But there is another side to our professional lives, our relationships with the adults with whom we work or with whom we have frequent contact: (a) the parents of the children, (b) our fellow-teachers, and (c) the supervisors to whom we are responsible.

Let's have a look at the parents first.

YOU AND THE PARENTS

The cooperative parent: How often has a mother stepped in and saved the day when a trip was planned and no one showed up to assist? Or a costume for a school play looked awful and her needle and thread worked magic? And there's the one who is never too busy to make a cake for a benefit sale, nor does she show annoyance when asked to serve on a PTA committee. What would we do without her?

I'll never forget one mother who went on a museum excursion with us. It was necessary to take the subway so we had planned each detail carefully and the children had set up a list of special safety rules. All went well until our return trip. When the train pulled into the crowded station I took my usual position in the doorway counting noses as the children entered the car while our mother brought up the rear. We were short two children!

"Alan and Joe are at the stand buying candy," announced the

last sheep to enter the fold. The subway car doors were closing. Our quick-thinking mother leaped through the narrow opening. "I'll stay with them," she called. "Don't worry!"

Five minutes after we arrived at our school the mother and two crestfallen boys showed up. Any teacher or parent knows the reaction, the desire to either smack them or hug them.

HOW DO WE FIND PARENTS WHO ARE WILLING TO ASSIST?

Any mother accompanying a class on an outing must be a person of goodwill or she wouldn't be bothered. Some are more alert to a situation and think more quickly in a crisis than others, but all of them take the job seriously.

As we read in "Planning with others" in Chapter 3 (*Planning Your Work*) a group of teachers working together compiled a list of mothers who were willing to go on trips with children. The list was made available to all grades. In addition, a notation was made of: (a) mothers who would volunteer to go only with their own children's classes, (b) mothers who would go with any grade, (c) mothers who would go in an emergency.

HOW PARENT AND TEACHER WORK TOGETHER DURING A TRIP

If it is possible, have a few minutes with the parent who is going with you a day or two before the trip. If you can't arrange this, write on a 3 by 5 card exactly what is expected of her. She'll appreciate it and feel more secure. Note such important details as:

1. Please stay at the end of the line when we are walking on the sidewalks or through the museum (or park, City Hall, etc.). In this way there will be no stragglers. (The teacher needs to be at the beginning of the line to find the way, watch for safe street crossings, etc.)

2. We have saved seat #9 for you the bus. (Teacher sits in the rear seat to supervise entire bus.)

3. Please don't permit any child to stand or move around in the bus, or to run in the museum, or along the sidewalk.

4. Thank you so much for giving us your day.

On the day following your excursion have your class officers write to the parent thanking her for her kindness: *Mail it.*

"CLASS MOTHERS"

Many schools have "Class Mothers" who assist at such times as evening conferences, teas, etc. They act as hostesses and see that conference time schedules are observed. These ladies are sometimes called upon to go on trips, too. "Class Mothers" are usually selected or volunteer through the Parents' Association.

OTHER KINDS OF COOPERATION

When a child is having difficulty in school the teacher frequently turns to the parents to try to find what's causing the trouble. It's usually the mother we see since few fathers are available when school is in session. How helpful it is when a parent arrives without a chip on her shoulder and with the earnest wish to cooperate. Even if all she says is, "What can *I* do?" at least she is there and will listen and try to help.

"SLAP-HAPPY BOBBY"

Bobby's classmates had christened him with a child's knack for choosing a nickname that hits the nail right on the head. His coat was always on the floor, the desk was a mare's nest, and the contents hadn't been sorted since school began. His papers were a horror; apple cores, paper clips, marbles, and chewed gum trailed him everywhere. There was no rhyme or reason for anything Bobby did, for he had no plans, aims, or system. But he was sweet tempered and likeable, and although his classmates teased him they were fond of him.

Miss Taylor's usual method for dealing with such a casual attitude had failed, and she thought it might help to talk with Bobby's mother. She tried to picture how the mother would look, but couldn't. The note went home (the second note, that is, for the first had disappeared) and an appointment was arranged for 3:05 on Tuesday.

At the exact moment an attractive woman, impeccably dressed, tapped on the door. It was Bobby's mother!

"I'm glad you asked me to come and talk with you," she said. "We seem to be having the same problem. Bobby thinks that as long as he's agreeable and smiling the world should make no further demands on him. Perhaps between us we can map out a campaign. I certainly appreciate your interest in him."

It was a welcome surprise for Miss Taylor. When a parent comes to you with such an attitude your battle with the child is half won.

FATHERS, TOO, CAN BE HELPFUL

So many fathers spend endless hours commuting to and from a job that they have little time or energy left for school problems. However, some of them are very good about attending concerts and shows in which their children take part—much to the joy of the children who get a real thrill out of peeking through the curtains and seeing Daddy in the audience. Occasionally a father will accept the position of president of the Parents' Association or PTA, but most of them are just too tired to take on such an assignment.

MR. KRESS HAD A DIFFERENT KIND OF SCHOOL PROBLEM

Not far from our school there is an interesting shop owned and run by a Mr. Kress where you can buy coins and stamps. The older children used to gather there on the way home and once in a while buy a coin or a stamp for an album. Most afternoons they would just congregate, laugh and giggle, and get in the way of customers. Mr. Kress was annoyed, but since he had a son and daughter about the age of these children he tried to be patient. He felt there must be an answer to the situation, but couldn't put his finger on it.

"TRY TURNING A SEEMING DISADVANTAGE INTO AN OPPORTUNITY"

One afternoon when the shop was overflowing with young ones a friend dropped in to chat. He was amused by Mr. Kress' attitude of ill-concealed annoyance.

"I'm surprised at you, Mike," he said. "Here's a golden opportunity dropped right in your lap and you're complaining!"

"Opportunity? This is an opportunity?" he asked. "I don't get it."

"Think it over, Mike," said his friend. "You'll get it."

Mr. Kress did think it over. He knew his friend did *not* mean that the children should be pressured into buying more stamps or coins, or even that he might declare the shop off limits. This friend was interested in psychology and liked to suggest, "Examine your problem from all sides and see how often a seeming disadvantage can be turned into an opportunity."

An idea began to take shape. Mr. Kress decided he would talk to his daughter's teacher.

PARENT AND TEACHER WORK OUT A PLAN

Here was the idea, still in embryo, that Mr. Kress presented to Susie's teacher. The children must be interested in coins and stamps or they wouldn't choose his shop to gather in. Right? Right! Would the school be willing for him to start a coin and stamp club or act as advisor to such a group if there already was a club? He might not be the world's greatest stamp expert, but he could help the members in their collecting and advise them about the best choices.

"Sounds good to me," said the teacher. "Let's go see Mr. Davis. He's in charge of our Stamp Club, but only because nobody volunteered. He often says he'd like to meet an expert who could give him some good advice and some ideas."

The details aren't important to our story, but the idea worked out successfully. Mr. Kress and Mr. Davis planned together so that the meetings were no longer mere stamp-pasting and coin-swapping sessions but educational gems. The shop in our town became a place where the stamp and coin buffs could meet, talk serious business, and find ready help and reference books on their hobby. It was the children themselves who discouraged their uninterested friends from making Mr. Kress' shop a hangout.

With Mr. Kress' knowledge of the subject and Mr. Davis' teaching experience the Stamp and Coin Club became a group of which the teachers and students were proud. Its activities were even reported in the town newspaper. Mr. Kress' former problem became a sort of blessing to him, to Mr. Davis, to the club members, and to the entire school because parent and teacher worked together to give their best.

THINGS THAT PARENTS COMPLAIN ABOUT

1. Homework: Nothing you do is going to please everybody, so let's not try. Homework probably causes more parental complaints than any other aspect of parent-child-teacher relationships. You receive a frenzied note from a parent telling of a child who stayed up half the night (?) to complete an assignment while another parent complains that you don't give enough homework. ("It keeps them off the streets, you know.")

Your school probably has its own policy about homework and suggests the proper amount for the various grades. This is the usual way in which the problem is handled because individual teachers vary so widely in how much they think should be given. (In France homework for young ones is forbidden by ministerial decree, although the children work very hard while in school and discipline is severe. When students enter the "Lycée" they are snowed under with homework, but not earlier.)

If there is no definite policy about the amount of homework to be given try to exercise good judgment and spread it out so that there's not too much to be done at once, *and* be sure children know when things are due. Then, if a child's snowed under at some time it's his own fault. *Above all, don't give punishment homework!*

2. Report cards: Too much importance is given to report cards and both teachers and parents are to blame. In almost any conference with a parent, whether it is about report cards or not, sooner or later the subject will come up.

Even though you may be given a standard by which to mark report cards each teacher interprets such a standard in his own way. Can you imagine the confusion that reigns in a household when three or four children bring home report cards on the same day? How can a parent possibly know what the marks represent? Is Jane smarter than brother Frank because she has an "A" in math and he has a "B"? How strict are the teachers who marked them? Some of us are known as "tough markers" and hand out "A's" or "Excellent's" or "Outstanding's" only on rare occasions.

Many school districts don't use A's and B's at all, nor do they use percentages. Instead there is a written statement for each subject explaining to the parents how their child stands in comparison with his classmates. This type of report is very rough on the teacher who not only spends countless hours preparing it but has to explain to each parent at conference time what it all means. The reaction of the parents is usually, "Why can't you use per cents? Those we understand, at least."

Use this technique in explaining the report to parents:

- Per cents are factual, yes. But how could you tell whether: (a) your child tried *very* hard to get that 75%; (b) your child is "coasting along" with a 75%; or (c) he crammed at the last minute to get 75% on a test after loafing and wasting time for days?

It's a new idea to most parents, but when they realize that the newer type of report card tries to evaluate their children as to how well they're working up to their ability, parents often take an increased interest in the progress report.

- Emphasize the importance of studying carefully the "Personality Traits" section of the card. This is meant to tell parents how their children are developing socially and *must never be considered less important than the rating in achievement.*

There are experimental schools that are trying out the idea of having no report cards. We shall have to wait until the results are in to see what the verdict will be.

3. "The school doesn't appreciate my child's ability": In Chapter Eight we discussed the fact that children are sometimes used by their parents to enhance the status of the family. It's unfortunate, but it does occur, and some communities are alive with this kind of rivalry. Sometimes it *is* possible for a bright child to remain undiscovered in the classroom, but he's usually the kind of child who has no wish to compete and who prefers to dream and "hide his light."

More often we find children with a sort of "flash in the pan" brightness which is easily mistaken for superior intelligence. When such a child is pinned down to facts he doesn't seem quite so smart. This is where parents are apt to be misled, for what parent wants to admit that his child is not unusual? There is always that fond hope—even in sensible parents. Some of them are better able to conceal the hope than others.

A MOST EXTRAORDINARY FATHER

Mr. Farber is a smart, quiet man, an architect. His only child, a daughter, is bright but lazy in school. Because of her high IQ she was placed in a rapid advance class.

The child was unhappy. She dreaded going to school each day, said she missed her old class, didn't like the new kids who, according to the girl, were showoff's.

Mrs. Farber is ambitious and anxious for her daughter to do well in school. The father is more concerned with the child's happiness than with the neighbors' approval or envy. Mother implored and scolded to make the child toe the mark. Dad stood by his daughter, maintaining that her happiness was more important. Finally he went to talk to the teacher.

To his mild surprise he discovered that the teacher was completely in accord with his own views. Daughter returned to her old classmates with no embarrassment and loved it.

"OLD-FASHIONED" PARENTS

In a town more countrylike than suburban, there is a hard-working couple with a large family. The girls are well trained by mother to cook, shop, do any kind of housework. The boys assist their father on weekends and holidays as he makes his rounds of neighborhood jobs.

The youngest of the group, Petey, had trouble learning to read. At the end of his third year in school the teacher sent for Dad to tell him that Petey might possibly be left back because of this difficulty. Dad had always maintained that Petey was the smartest of the lot, but didn't argue the point with the teacher.

"If Petey can't read good," said Dad, "he's got no right being promoted. If you think leaving him back will help, you leave him back."

Petey *was* left back, and he *did* learn to read.

HANDLING INTERVIEWS AND CONFERENCES

Years ago it was almost unheard of for a parent to go to see the teacher. Unless there was something pretty bad going on a father wouldn't be found dead in his child's classroom. Then it began to change—gradually, at the beginning, with invitations to attend assembly programs, then "Come and visit us during Open School Week," and finally with series of conferences both during school hours and in the evening so all parents would be able to come.

A great many problems have been created by this newer idea but many more problems have been solved. Anyway, it's a waste of time for a teacher to complain about it, and the smart thing to do is to handle the conference or interview capably so that time is not wasted on either side.

THE "REQUEST" INTERVIEW

When you request it: You may need a parent's cooperation in the handling of some problem with her child. Write her a simple, concise note asking if she can come at a definite time on a certain day, and if she cannot will she please tell you when it will be possible. In fairness to the mother give her at least an inkling of what's going on but refrain from writing an epistle of her child's shortcomings. Don't send home the note via another child. If the child himself is unlikely to give it to mother, mail it.

Be well prepared for the interview. Reread the child's case history, writing your notes on a 3 by 5 card. Jot down, also, exactly the ground you hope to cover with the parent, and what you expect to tell her, *and* what you plan to ask her to do.

When she arrives, be courteous and restrained in your comments. After all, she probably loves her child and you'll gain nothing by hurting her feelings. Let her know immediately that you appreciate her interest and will not keep her long for you know she's a busy woman. (This will remind her that you, too, are a busy person and may tend to restrain a rambling or long-winded parent.)

At the close of the interview go over the salient points with her (pencil and card in hand—it makes a lasting impression). Repeat briefly the plans you two have made. Thank her for coming.

When the parent requests it: Answer the request the same day and set a time for the interview. Then get busy and prepare yourself. Take another 3 by 5 card and go through the case history in your records. Then check your own record book for marks (and remarks) making notes as you proceed. If the parent has told you why she wants to come, so much the better. In either case, have your notes ready and let the mother see that you have such details at your fingertips. This impresses the parent with your interest in the child and shows that you mean business.

SCHOOLWIDE CONFERENCE TIME

In many school districts there is a conference time set aside for personal interviews with parents. These are rather frequent in kindergarten through the second grade and subside to twice a year in higher grades. Each parent is asked whether she (we hope fathers can make it too) prefers an afternoon or an evening appointment and is then assigned a definite period (from 10 to 20 minutes long, depending on the rush). Children are excused at noon on conference day and parents do surprisingly well with the keeping of their appointments.

Save your own time and any possible embarrassment by preparing a card for each child. Fathers are especially impressed with this procedure and see it is not a time for the mutual admiration of the child but a time to get results. Make an occasional note while conferring with the parent. If you have a library table in the room, sit there. Seeing the teacher at the desk and feeling like a 10-year-old doesn't help a parent to relax, but sitting around a table establishes a better climate.

OPEN SCHOOL WEEK

This is rough! But it's part of being a teacher, so accept it with as good grace as possible. Some schools (bless their hearts) set a scheduled time for the parents of each grade to visit the classes while in session. Other schools declare an open season for the entire week. In both cases the school is open one evening for parent-teacher conferences.

You know all about the importance of having an attractive room, but be sure you have the children's work on display. Try to have *something* done by each child somewhere in sight. Have a folder on each desk—a folder containing his papers, good, bad, or indifferent—a folder decorated as the owner sees fit. Encourage his parents to study it.

PARENTS ARE PEOPLE, TOO

During your years of teaching you will meet all kinds of parents. There may be those who consider you a natural enemy, perhaps as a result of an unfortunate encounter with an unreasonable teacher. You can assure him or her by your actions and attitude that this doesn't apply to you.

You will meet parents who will try flattery. Show them that you don't need it or wish it. There will be an occasional parent who just won't come, or won't cooperate. Do what you can to confer with this kind without making a nuisance of yourself. You may have to deal with him (or her) through the school nurse, or as a last resort a command appearance from the principal.

Most parents are reasonable. Most of them want to do what is best for the child. Most of them will go along with you if they know you care.

OUR FELLOW TEACHERS

In any group of people working together whether it is in an office, a school, a club, or a church you will find those who are devoted to the cause and those who tend to "soldier" on the job, you will find loners and the socially minded, the bossy and the meek, an occasional rabble-rouser, and some who are as near to the angels as one could get.

College degrees don't change people basically. Teachers are people too. We don't see as much of each other as we would in a business office for we spend so much of our time closeted with children and most of our problems are concerned with them. It is important, nevertheless, that we are able to meet, and talk with, and associate with our fellow teachers—it's important to our work, and important to ourselves.

In Chapter 3 we looked into the need of working with others on the same grade and the many advantages to be gained by doing this. Planning to share material, to put on a joint entertainment, to discuss problems peculiar to that grade or problems that concern the whole school—all these are much better when discussed with co-workers than in trying to go it alone.

Some lasting friendships are begun in schools, no one has to tell you about these. But let's talk about problems that arise when people work together; about the need for giving that extra bit and being able to take it too; about the need to understand frayed nerves in tired people and the hope that they will understand ours.

WHY "FRAYED NERVES"?

Teaching has never been a cinch. Have you ever tried to picture some of your nonteacher friends coping with just *one* of the problems you are apt to meet in an ordinary school day (a friend who talks too much about your "short" working hours, or your vacations, even your pay)? Wouldn't this friend be indignant if he were expected to sacrifice lunchtime, or evenings, or vacations as part of the job?

It is impossible for one who is not a teacher to imagine the strain of handling numbers of children for hours on end. We expect to do that and don't complain. It's the extras that have been piled on us very gradually through the years that have brought us to the breaking point. We are rarely asked if we are willing to do these things, the new responsibilities are added to the others as nonchalantly as you would add more pounds to the load on the back of a pack mule. The mule has the prerogative of balking or kicking.

HOW DID ALL THIS GET STARTED?

Way, way back few children brought their lunch to school and little supervision was needed at lunchtime. Then the government-subsidized lunch for poorly fed children was begun and gradually expanded until 60 to 90 per cent of pupils (some paid, some free) now eat lunch in school. They have to be supervised, so it's up to the teachers.

With the disappearance of the little red schoolhouse and the building of huge "central schools" bus service became a necessity, and teachers have to meet these buses in the morning and see them off in the afternoon. Even in cities a great many children travel by school bus.

Duty schedules reached ridiculous proportions. A person is educated to teach, trained through the years to become more effective, and his strength and good nature are dissipated in high-priced baby-sitting. Every privilege granted to the pupils drains that much more from the education everyone is so anxious for them to receive.

IS ANYTHING BEING DONE ABOUT IT?

Yes! Boards of Education are alarmed at the number of teachers leaving the school systems each year. Many of these teachers would rather stay with the job, but they can't take it any longer. Finally the message has gotten through, but results are slow in coming.

Mothers have volunteered to do some of the clerical and baby-sitting jobs to ease the burden, but often the children won't mind them and sometimes bedlam reigns. So even if their help was and is appreciated there are certain areas where only teachers are able to control large numbers of children.

TEACHER'S AIDES

Just as Nurses' Aides came to the rescue when the graduate nurses' burden became too great. Teachers' Aides are now appearing on the scene. Most of these Aides are women who have the necessary requirements, live nearby, and are pleased to make some extra money by spending a few hours each day assisting in lunchrooms, libraries, and the school office.

Teachers are still needed to supervise lunch periods and bus arrivals and departures, but one teacher and some Aides can take the place of the three or four teachers needed previously. This lightens the burden on the staff and is a tremendous help. There seems to be a growing tendency to treat the teacher as fairly as any other skilled worker, to let him spend more of his time doing what he was trained to do, and not waste it on tiring chores that someone else is quite pleased to take over.

OTHER WAYS IN WHICH TEACHERS' AIDES ARE HELPING

There are innumerable other duties that were once considered part of the teacher's job, such as selling cookies and milk and keeping a strict account of all these miniature sales, banking for the students, collecting for nationwide or community drives, typing and mimeographing, making arrangements for speakers to appear at assemblies, sending for and arranging for the use of museum materials and special exhibits. You can add to the list, for it's endless.

Surprisingly, the Aides are showing us that with a little guidance they can do these chores very efficiently. I don't know why we should be surprised, for most of these Aides are intelligent women and enjoy doing it. There are still plenty of extracurricular jobs that must be done by teachers, such as marking tests and recording marks, acting as counselors to our children, appearing at and taking part in community activities, participating in professional activities, and a host of others. But for many of us the burden is more bearable than it has been in years.

HOW CAN TEACHERS HELP EACH OTHER?

You can't teach your neighbor's class, you can't take over your neighbor's clerical duties, it would be unwise to take your neighbor's yard or lunch duty (except under unusual circumstances), but there are things that we can do for each other and they are a great boost to morale.

VICKIE'S SENSE OF HUMOR

Vickie has her troubles, too. She rarely mentions them, but she will always listen to yours. By the time you've finished a recital of the way the world (educational, that is) has been treating you, why, suddenly you're laughing and not nearly as weary. She has a way with a phrase, or a wisecrack, or a salty comment. Vickie doesn't offer advice, but somehow you don't feel the need of it after talking to her.

Not many of us have this gift, but all of us can listen to our co-workers, let them blow off steam in a harmless way, and *keep our mouths shut afterwards!* Nothing causes more damage to professional relationships than carrying tales told in confidence.

A LITTLE "WAITING ON"

Have you had the experience of coming upstairs from duty in the noisy, crowded lunchroom and finding your place set at the table in the teachers' room and the kettle boiling? It's a small thing, but a taste of heaven. Or perhaps you've been out in the playground in the hot sun for your stint of yard duty and dread the thought of picking up the burden for the afternoon, and find that some angel has prepared a tall, icy glass of tea or coffee for you. A thoughtful gesture like this can mean just about everything.

BE ON TIME

When you are expected to be in the lunchroom or in the yard to relieve the teacher who has been on duty, *be prompt.* Every second of that last three minutes on duty is a small lifetime. It was always a stroke of luck to be teamed up with Mrs. Lott, for she had the reputation of appearing at least one minute early. Sounds a little silly? No, you try it and see.

If there is a short grade conference planned for 12:30 or 3:05, *be on time* so the meeting can get started and finished. If one of the group is late the time of the others is wasted in briefing the late arrival on what he has missed.

SHARE THE WEALTH

Miss De Brae, the unofficial music teacher in one rather small school, would be asked to hunt up a song in her music books, or a record needed for any class entertaining in the assemblies, go over a new song with an unmusical teacher, even to stay late or come early to rehearse for an event. She could be depended upon to comply smilingly. No one else on the staff could do it, but she could, and enjoyed it, although it sometimes required more than she had the time or energy to contribute.

Mr. Jahn has a knack with appliances of any kind. It seems that he spends most of his lunch hours mending the teachers' radios, tape recorders or filmstrip projectors so they can use them that very afternoon. He never objects, and I fear we sometimes take advantage of his good nature.

If you have found some new material that you can share with your grade, or material that a teacher in another grade might use profitably, don't hug it to your bosom, but let it be used where it will do the most good.

A bit of forethought, a touch of kindness, a smile instead of a groan, can go far toward making any school more pleasant. If this sounds like the Golden Rule, well, what's wrong with that?

STUDENT TEACHERS

It's unfair to take a young teacher fresh from college and toss her (or him) to the lions. Any aspiring teacher has the right to be trained in the best possible way and books can't do the whole job. Nothing compares with the help a veteran teacher can give *right in the classroom*. You can talk child psychology, discipline, and methods for years and a young teacher will still be unprepared to face the realities of day-by-day teaching. Teaming up with an experienced, practical person and working and teaching under this person's guidance is almost as necessary as internship to a young doctor.

SOME STUDENT TEACHERS ARE "NATURALS"

It's not always easy or convenient to take a student teacher into your classroom and give the young person the necessary guidance. I recall one spring term some years ago when we were told by Headquarters to prepare an inventory of every blessed thing in the building. This was the kind of order sometimes given by one in authority who has forgotten, or never experienced, what the addition of another burden means to teachers. The assignment turned out to be more onerous than we had dreamed possible.

At the same time a young woman from a neighboring college was assigned to me as a student teacher. It seemed too much to bear at first, but she proved to be a rare jewel. She struck exactly the right note with the children, loved to teach, and had a good sense of discipline (so often lacking in the inexperienced). She caught on to our procedures almost effortlessly, prepared her lessons, coached the slow readers, was anxious to improve, and accepted any criticism graciously.

After a time I could leave her with the children for an hour now and then and feel certain that she would have the situation well in hand when I returned. This gave me an opportunity to visit supply closets and check the endless inventory. When the data was gathered she offered to run off the figures on an adding machine and asked for the privilege of typing the whole business. What a blessing she was!

When this young lady left us after several months the children were desolate. They secretly bought her a present and there were some tears, both hers and theirs, when the "Goodbyes" were said. She kept in touch with us and when she graduated decided to accept an appointment in a so-called problem school. She's a "natural" if I ever saw one.

THOSE WHO NEED MORE HELP

Not every student teacher has what it takes to make a good classroom teacher. You can usually tell in your day-by-day contact with them whether or not they care about the need for practical experience, whether or not they are interested in children. You almost feel you could prophesy whether or not they'll keep on teaching or merely use it as a stepping-stone to something less arduous.

There are many others who will become good teachers if the proper guidance and some encouragement are given to them. Perhaps you will be the one who can influence the course a young person will take. Maybe he or she will never be a brilliant teacher, but sympathy, understanding, and diligence are more important than brilliance.

HOW TO HELP YOUR STUDENT TEACHER

1. Be a friend: Don't force the student teacher to confide in you, but be willing to listen. There may be problems that you have long forgotten that seem insurmountable to a young person.

2. What are her interests? Is there something *she* can contribute to the class, something *he* can do well? A good singing voice, a love of music, art, poetry? Can she tell stories to the children? Is he good at games?

3. Help them plan: Go over your plan book with the student teacher. Explain, simply, your long range and immediate plans so she knows what's going on. Show him how you put these plans to work in the classroom.

Let her plan for a period of 20 minutes (at first) with the slow readers. Let him work out a simple problem in math with the children.

4. Hard facts too: Take them with you occasionally when you are on lunch or yard duty or that bus assignment. It would be unfair to pretend such things don't exist.

5. Praise when you can. Be patient when necessary.

6. Don't criticize the school.

7. Be frank in your criticism of a lesson, but never show amusement at a clumsy procedure. Suggest a better alternative—but in private, naturally.

Your good sense will tell you many more do's and don'ts as you proceed from day to day with these young teachers.

We are warned about permitting the student teacher and the children to get too involved with each other. I have noticed there is a natural rapport between some trainees and the pupils, and absolutely none where others are concerned. It seems to me that this takes care of itself. The affection enriches everyone, the lack of it is either unnoticed or forgotten immediately.

YOU AND YOUR SUPERVISORS

An elementary school is usually small enough to have just one supervisor, the principal. Rarely is it as large as a junior high where there may be one or more assistants, and possibly departmental chairmen also. Let's talk about the principal of your school, and if you have other supervisors the same suggestions should work there too.

A principal once said to me, "A supervisor's life is very lonely." When I seemed to question the statement she added, "We must not appear too friendly with anyone in the school, for that would be unwise. If we seem cold we are disliked. And frankly we don't have enough time left over to make and keep friendships on the outside."

MOST PRINCIPALS WORK HARD

How often have you passed the quiet, cool office on your way in from the playground with a sweaty, excited group of 30, or 40, or 50 softball players and envied the peace enjoyed by the principal? But you didn't know about the hysterical parent who took half the afternoon, or the sick child whose mother was finally located, or the stack of reports to be read before he leaves the building, or the superintendent's meeting called for 4:15 PM. All of these are part of your principal's day, and like you he is continually having new responsibilities thrust upon him. To whom will *he* kick?

He's usually available when you need him, isn't he? Listens to your beefs? Worries about your class if you're out sick? He may have his shortcomings, but he tries hard to do a good job.

"NO LIFE OF MY OWN"

Just as teachers have had more and more duties piled on them, the principal's life has become more and more complicated with endless reports. There's Miss Ellison, for example.

She was a peppy, excellent teacher. Work never fazed her and she continued to study winter and summer for the degrees that would make her eligible to take the necessary exams for the privilege of becoming a principal, something she wanted very much.

She became the principal of a small, rather shopworn school, but that didn't bother her, she loved the work. After a few years she moved to a new building, and that was fine too. Then the dream began to fade. Her friends had to give up asking her to join them for an evening. The theater had to be foregone. The toughest blow came when she sold her beloved weekend place because she never got there and it was becoming rundown from neglect.

After a few years Miss Ellison was forced to retire because of ill health. The job she wanted so much proved too tough to handle, and one more hardworking, devoted principal was lost to the schools.

SHOULD A TEACHER TRY TO HELP?

Why not? To take a practical rather than a sympathetic view of it, if you can do something to help, your supervisor will be less harried and have more time and more patience left for his teachers.

> 1. If a plan book is required, and that's usually so, have it in the office at the stipulated time.
> 2. Get your reports in on time and see that they're accurate.
> 3. Don't send discipline problems to him except in an emergency. Discipline is *your* job and nine times out of ten you can handle it on the spot.
> 4. When he comes to watch you teach (that's *his* job) smile if it kills you and go right ahead with your lesson.

WHEN THINGS DON'T GO SMOOTHLY

There are bound to be times when a teacher feels unappreciated, "put-upon," even abused. You feel the principal has been unfair in his assignments of duty, or you've been given the third miserable class in a row. Why should you put up with such treatment when so-and-so is treated like a delicate flower? Yes, most of us feel this way or worse every now and then. Maybe we're more tired than usual, and it's also possible that we're *not* being treated with the consideration due us.

Is it better to broadcast your griefs far and wide or do the sensible thing?

A TALK WITH THE PRINCIPAL IS IN ORDER

1. Don't rush into his office unexpected and red-faced with annoyance.

2. Calm down and do some thinking. Sleep on it.

3. If you feel you are in the right and have a case, do some homework.

4. Write down the facts. It not only make a favorable impression, but will save you the embarrassment of forgetting what you want most to say.

5. Rehearse your part.

6. Write to the principal, briefly and politely, asking to see him.

7. State your case as you rehearsed it without recriminations or accusations of favoritism.

8. Maintain your dignity at all costs. Speak quietly.

9. Whatever happens, don't cry (girls); don't lose your temper (boys).

10. Give your principal a chance to explain the situation. He should have *that* right! In most instances a solution can be worked out and you'll both feel better for having cleared the air.

THE FINEST PRINCIPAL I EVER KNEW

A real lady, but not afraid to take on an irate parent or an aggrieved teacher. A real fighter who never lost her temper. Sympathetic and understanding, but neither child nor adult ever tried to get away with anything when under her supervision. All of us wanted to please her although she never make any extraordinary demands upon us. She went to bat for her teachers and warded off many a blow meant for us.

Now that she has "retired" what is she doing? She's still fighting battles, but now she champions retired teachers, travels back and forth to and from the state capital urging backing for the passage of bills giving retired teachers new benefits, writes letters to congressmen and newspapers.

She has never lost her zest for a good fight in a good cause. She enjoys her new life and has fine memories of the old one. All her former teachers and many of her former students "arise up and call her blessed."

— GETTING ALONG WITH THE ADULTS —
IN OUR PROFESSIONAL LIVES

A teacher must know how to work well with: a) parents, b) fellow teachers, and c) supervisors.

Most parents will cooperate with you. They help you on field trips, try to help solve their children's school problems, appear at conferences, and visit when invited.

The things parents most often complain about are: a) homework, b) report cards, c) and the seeming unappreciation of their children's abilities. These questions or complaints can be handled at conference times. Prepare yourself beforehand by studying records and facts.

In any kind of interview or conference with a parent have the facts you wish to cover written on a 3 by 5 card.

In working with fellow teachers try to keep in mind that they, like you, are often tired and pushed beyond endurance. Any small, thoughtful act on your part will help to lighten the work load and ease tensions created by too many duties and too much pressure.

Teachers' Aides are coming into the schools to help in clerical and other non-teaching jobs that have been so time-consuming.

Student teachers can work with class and teacher so that all parties profit from the relationship.

Dealing with children comes more naturally to some student teachers, but others can learn by practical experience in the classroom and by the practical, friendly advice and guidance of a veteran teacher.

Your principal also carries a heavy work load and is under much pressure. It will help everyone concerned if your reports are accurate and on time, if your plan book is turned in when it is due, and if you take care of your own disicplinary problems, except in rare instances.

Chapter Twelve

Looking Ahead at Education

*E*ducation is being forced to keep pace with a world in a state of rapid change. Ideas are coming thick and fast. Some are tried and quickly fizzle out; others are proving their worth and are being incorporated into the "system." Still others are on the way.

Let's look into some of the newer trends, plans, and actual doings of modern education.

DECENTRALIZATION OF SCHOOLS

The school systems of most of our large cities are so huge they are unable to operate efficiently. We hear them spoken of as "monolithic, a massive whole of solid uniformity without diversity or variation," and "bureaucracies whose administrative and policy-making groups are marked by lack of initiative and flexibility." Perhaps the word "flexibility" is the key to the problem for it is the almost complete absence of it that so hinders the operation of these big city systems.

A colossus moves slowly but the barbs are getting sharper and the colossus is beginning to move. Plans long formulated and unused are being revised and tried. It boils down to this—large school systems must be decentralized to operate effectively.

WHAT DOES THIS MEAN?

It means that there must be a delegation of power to smaller districts. "Centralization of authority" no longer works. Whether the newly formed districts will be boroughs, or a former school district, or a single community, or an educational "park" will vary from city to city, but a change is overdue.

There is a great deal of talk (and *some* action) about community school districts. A community feels it knows more about the problems of educating its own youth than the vast, impersonal city complex does.

How might such an arrangement work? Could such problems as new curricula, appointments of teachers, salaries, buying of supplies, maintenance, be handled competently in a community unaccustomed to so much sudden power? Many think "Yes," because the local school board, the parents, and the community leaders know their own people and are acquainted with the problems and needs of their own area.

The large cities could take a page from the experience of their surrounding suburban neighbors who operate school districts where children number several thousand instead of hundreds of thousands, districts where the parents vote on issues that pertain only to their own schools and where there is a sharp awareness and interest in those schools.

This we know: The monolithic Boards of Education as we have known them are in for a change.

EDUCATIONAL PARKS

There was a movement some years ago to get away from the overly large public school and to erect buildings in specific neighborhoods. These schools came to be called "neighborhood schools." Parents' Associations, principals, and teachers were proud of their schools and everyone worked together to provide their children with the best in equipment and privileges.

More recently the value of the neighborhood school has been questioned. Critics say that children who receive their early education in them are blind to the rest of society, don't know "how the other half lives," form prejudices that hurt them when they must attend a large high school. Parents in such neighborhoods are often bitter about the attempts at more integration. They can't see why their children should be bused away to attend a school in a different kind of community.

It is not our purpose here to offer a solution. New ideas have been developed and rejected, but one that is very much alive is that of the "Educational Parks." What are they? Are they schools set in parklike surroundings to give city children a taste of the beautiful? Not at all!

A COMPLEX OF EDUCATIONAL FACILITIES

Many plans have been drawn up, many "parks" designed, and all have some features in common. Generally the park has facilities for children from first grade through high school. There are separate buildings for each level; for example, three elementary schools housing about 500 children each, possibly two junior highs, each accommodating 700 (more or less), a high school for 1,500 or so, and perhaps a junior college too. There is a centrally located section of the park where the recreational and research facilities for the whole complex are situated, convenient to all buildings.

Other parks are planned to include public housing projects and evening facilities for adults, and all the resources of the park complex will be available to students and other residents evenings, weekends, and vacation times.

Advantages to teachers are being stressed too. Team teaching and nongraded classes will be more feasible with this new all-in-one grouping of the various levels of education. There are many more teachers to draw upon—experts in teaching slow learners, or the gifted child; science specialists, musicians, artists.

Then, too, the facilities for team teaching would be greatly increased, for in a large complex like an educational park it is possible to have modern equipment such as computers, talking typewriters, libraries of film and tape to be used by all the schools in the park. This would be prohibitively expensive in a single school, but in a "park" it could be housed for the convenience of all and would serve thousands of people.

NOVA SCHOOL, FORT LAUDERDALE

One of the first educational complexes is in Fort Lauderdale, Florida—not in the city proper, but out in the "cow pastures." It is in actual operation and includes all grades from pre-kindergarten to junior college, and expects to include a graduate school in the future. Here we find team teaching, nongraded classes, and independent study (the child decides when he's ready to be tested for advancement to the next level). There are no report cards for elementary children.

This is an experiment and has been operating several years. The students and staff have great faith in its future.

OTHER CITIES PLAN EDUCATIONAL PARKS

"Park" enthusiasts in Washington, D.C., would like to have a ring of educational parks around the city. In this way Washington, although surrounded by suburbs, would draw its students from both the city and nearby communities. New York City is already using new schools which will one day be part of park complexes. There is a nationwide interest in these projects. One busy town near a large city in New Jersey is building a "park" on its borders that will draw its students from both the city and the town.

One reason for the interest in this plan is the greater facility offered for the integration of children. Another is the actual dollar saving in the operation of large complexes as against many small buildings.

Educational parks are praised by enthusiasts and roundly criticized by skeptics. "Too expensive!" "A waste of money!" "Unrealistic!" say some. "Look at the possibilities for integration!" say others, "and at the same time they offer educational advantages for children such as we have never known."

TEAM TEACHING

Team teaching seems like such a sensible idea that one wonders why it isn't more generally used. Here the "master teacher" is in charge of a small group of teachers—advising, guiding the planning of the others, acting as the easily accessible head of a small number of co-workers. The one who is best fitted to teach a given subject teaches it to all the classes in the group (usually on the same grade, but not necessarily).

How realistic it is to have everyone taught by the person best qualified to handle a specific subject, whether it's music or art, science or math, whether he has a way with slow children, or knows how to challenge the lazy, possibly bored bright child—in each case he's working where he's tops.

From the teacher's point of view, aside from the satisfaction of doing that for which one is best fitted, there is another advantage.

Team teaching goes a long way toward rescuing teachers from the isolation so common to our work. You are a member of a group which meets frequently to discuss plans and problems, a group which shares the responsibility for the education of 100 or more children. Ideas are exchanged with others in the group, all of whom are interested in the same students and deeply involved with them. A behavior problem? Someone in the group may have found the answer to it. Subject matter to be taught? An innovation to be tried out? Talk it over, Talk it out, as advocates of group therapy advise. Teachers need this. We work alone too much. In team teaching the responsibilities are shared, although each member is definitely responsible for his own subject (or subjects).

Of course, most of our school buildings were not erected with team teaching in mind. Where would a member of a teaching team meet with just three students for some special work? Or 15 students? Or 75? (The size of groups may vary greatly from time to time.) Actually, some such accommodations *can* be found in almost any school building and they don't have to be 100 per cent ideal for you to use them to good advantage. As far as the physical setup is concerned, team teaching could be started in many school districts tomorrow. Unfortunately, it takes some mental adjustment on the part of school boards, supervisors—and teachers, too. But it's on its way.

NONGRADED CLASSES

Team teaching and nongraded classes seem to have been made for each other. They work well separately but let's see how neatly they fit into the same teaching setup.

Each child reports to his homeroom teacher who is responsible for his overall progress. Here we find children of about the same age level, but the similarity to an ordinary classroom ends soon. Each child's program develops and changes to fit his own needs. With the nongraded plan a child may be doing the equivalent of fifth year reading very acceptably but joins a fourth year level for his math. A child in the fourth year who is bright in science is more at home with a sixth year level science group. Ideally, in the nongraded school children advance in each subject at their own rate and the fear of failure that stalks so many of them is largely eliminated.

The math specialist is better able to cope with the difficulty that is holding back one child. The science teacher can challenge the younger child with experiments and projects, listen more intelligently to his questions, give him appropriate problems to be solved. Youngsters are neither held back to listen in boredom to their less gifted classmates, nor are they on the other hand so discouraged by the losing battle of "keeping up" that they stop trying.

CURRICULA ARE CHANGING

In a world that is moving ahead with such relentless speed it is a difficult matter for any profession to keep pace. What is new today may be "old hat" tomorrow. In a system as steeped in tradition as education things have always moved slowly and the giant is somewhat befuddled as he is prodded into action, but he's trying. The superintendent of schools of one of our large cities has asked his teachers to experiment with new ideas in the classroom. He says mistakes may be made but the gains will far outweigh the losses. He wants to hear from lively, innovative teachers and he wants them to feel free of fear of retribution. Such a thing would have been earthshaking not too long ago!

No doubt there will always be curricula of some kind or other, but many of our old, familiar ones are due for some changes as educators try to meet the changing environment.

MODERN MATH

The shock of the modern math program has worn off and teachers have accepted it, grudgingly at first, but more willingly as they see the progress and interest shown by children.

Now we are told that this is only the beginning of a whole new series of math concepts. Modern children will have to be taught many more kinds of math. But take what comfort you can from another statement which tells us that not all children will be ready to assimilate this, nor will all children have need of it. Not all teachers are math-minded enough to handle such highly technical subjects, and that type of teaching will have to be done by trained specialists.

In spite of all the changes taking place in math curricula teachers are in general agreement that there is still a need for drill in the fundamentals. We had expected at first that some miracle of modern procedure might eliminate this, but such has not been the case. Don't be afraid to drill *when drill is needed.* It is not only of immense practical value to the child but is a great little character builder too.

SCIENCE IN THE CLASSROOM

In the age of spaceships, hydrogen bombs, and moon explorations our little nature study lessons might seem out of step. But let's not forget the joy a child finds in examining a leaf, a nest, a frog (as we stressed in Chapter Four, "The wonder in the 'near-at-hand' ") for this is science too.

Learning about the moon and stars, following the adventures of astronauts and moon explorations, becoming acquainted with the secrets of outer space, is part of the new science that teachers are learning along with the children. It is important that we guide our students intelligently in these new fields and keep abreast of such current happenings which no science curriculum can possibly foresee.

Each has its place in our science lessons. Children have every right to inquire into the wonders of space and feel a great need to study their own backyards.

INDUCTIVE TEACHING

This is nothing new for it has always been the way in which a thinking teacher tried to train the young. Educators of the "newer school" agree that inductive teaching, intelligently presented, prepares children to discover things for themselves instead of remembering thousands of unconnected, uninteresting facts that seem to have no relationship to their lives. To "know the answer" will no longer be enough for tomorrow's citizen. He must be taught in the school to weigh the facts, to see their significance in handling real life problems. The teacher presents the problem, whether it is in math, science, or social studies, and leads the class in the thinking that will help them solve it. In teaching children to use the inductive approach it is up to the instructor to present a well thought out problem and help the children to "discover" the solution, and incidently (and most importantly) to discover the pleasure and satisfaction gained from this way of attacking a problem.

SOCIAL STUDIES

There is an increasing amount of pressure being used to change the social studies curriculum as we now know it. Ethnic groups in large cities want to see more emphasis placed on the contributions of their people in the development of the United States. These groups maintain that minority children need a background with which they can identify; they need to be proud of something instead of feeling that they don't belong. Rather than learning about the background, history, and achievements of the majority they would study the historical and geographical background of their own ancestors.

It seems reasonable that children in underprivileged areas should have a curriculum more fitted to their special needs. We have been trying to start every child at the same place in social studies and math and science, and have expected each of them to assimilate whatever we give him in the same way. Only the teacher who has worked with children in deprived areas knows how wrong we have been.

This idea might be tried out in small, appropriate areas of a city if decentralization goes that far. How successful the plan would be remains to be seen. We might hazard a guess that after a time the pendulum would swing to some kind of compromise curriculum.

BRINGING IN SPECIALISTS TO THE SCHOOLS

Councils of educators, scientists, musicians, and language experts meeting to discuss the curricula of the new era emphasize the importance of bringing in talented outsiders to help the schools in the teaching of their specialties. Musicians, for example, who have less than full-time jobs in orchestras could be invited to give concerts, or teach a few classes a week, or give group or individual instruction in the violin, piano, singing—for pay, of course. Scientists from nearby universities would lend their knowledge and talents to children in grade schools in much the same way as it is done in educational parks.

To make social studies more real visitors from foreign lands might appear in costume to present dances and songs, talk about living and working in India, Norway, Japan, the countries of Africa. Officials of the city or the immediate community could talk with the classes about problems of government that concern children.

A newspaper reporter, a poet, a struggling writer or artist, amateurs as far as teaching is concerned, all of these may someday be invited to our schools to inspire the children at firsthand. We have not *begun* to tap our local resources for the education of the young. Formal learning is due for some big changes.

SEX EDUCATION

Long overdue, there is now a danger that sex education may be pushed into the schools too fast. It's been a topic that school boards, principals, and teachers have fought shy of. There's been a great deal of passing the buck from one to the other: "The home should teach it!"; "The school should take on the responsibility!"; "It's up to the church!" In the meantime children go on being uninformed or misinformed.

Suddenly the schools seem to realize that it is indeed up to them. But who is qualified to teach it? Who will "bell the cat"? Not every teacher is ready to do the job, for if sex education is not taught wisely it is better not done at all. Some schools are selecting teachers to take in-service courses that will aid them in the task, for it is not an easy one. An untrained teacher is apt to show uneasiness with a class and the cause is lost. Or he may be apt to get too clinical and the children aren't ready for that approach.

Do we start with the little ones and make it part of their family living unit in social studies? If so, what do we do with the nine- to twelve-year-olds who need the instruction? If children have had no guidance to date, what happens? Do we start with a "BANG!" and give them too much at once?

The problem is being faced, anyway, and it's high time. Let's hope that trained, confident teachers are given the job of handling sex education in their schools.

THE ITA ALPHABET AS AN AID TO READING

The Initial Teaching Alphabet was invented by Sir James Pitman, grandson of the inventor of shorthand. There are 44 characters, each standing for a single sound, and they cover every sound in the English language.

Although the ITA alphabet has been in use a comparatively

short time it is enjoying increasing popularity and success every year. Smaller school districts experimented with it before the larger cities for they have to go through less red tape in any experiment. First grade children are taught the new alphabet *before* they learn the regulation 26 letters so there is no confusing problem of "unlearning." Usually one first grade class in a school is selected while the other first grades are taught reading in the old, familiar way.

One teacher who resented "all this nonsense" says now that she can't find anything to complain about: "It's perfect! When it gives little children such a feeling of independence that they can pick up a new book and *read* it; when they can write their own little stories without constantly running to me for help; you can hardly praise it too highly."

Suburban schools that have been working with the ITA alphabet are extending its use to all their first grades and continue using it through the third year. One of the big questions raised by teachers and parents is about the transition the child must make to the 26 letter alphabet. Oddly enough this turns out to be no problem at all, for the change is made effortlessly, almost instantaneously. Teachers find spelling ability increased, and the greater facility with words the ITA alphabet fosters lends confidence to all their work.

TRAINING FOR TEACHING

Education has been subject to some pretty frank criticism lately and much of it is deserved. What the critics may not realize is that people in the system have been saying the same thing for years, but they were "voices crying in the wilderness" and although they knew whereof they spoke, no one listened.

The wide sale of books on the subject has brought the problem to every doorstep—suddenly all the voters are experts. In a changing world education seems to them to be static.

Every phase of education is being examined by experts and novices, and countless suggestions and demands made. Schools have been made the scapegoat for all the ills of the nation from poor reading to losing the space race. But experts in the know point a finger at teacher training as being the place to start improving the situation.

WHAT IS WRONG WITH TEACHER TRAINING?

Ask the young people coming out of college and entering the schools as teachers at the rate of about 200,000 a year! "I had to waste my time on courses I didn't need!" "I wanted courses that were not available!" "I never set foot in a classroom until I was tossed into my own!" "If only I could have done more practice teaching!" "Too many 'methods' courses," or not enough. "Too much liberal arts," or too little. Not all colleges make the same mistakes, but the graduates have one complaint in common—"I didn't feel prepared to teach!" Something must be wrong.

Certainly liberal arts courses are needed in the education of teachers and methods are a must. But teachers old and young agree that actual teaching experience in the classroom is, as we said in Chapter 10, almost as necessary as an internship to the young doctor. First, observing the experienced teacher at work, then working with her side by side on the firing line; teaching under her guidance; finally handling classes for an hour, two hours, a morning on one's own. Talking with the veteran; making mistakes and finding the answers to them—nothing can take the place of this kind of training.

OBSERVING REAL LIFE SITUATIONS

There are two more very practical ways in which modern teachers' colleges are preparing their students for the day they enter classrooms, either as an apprentice or as a teacher on combat duty:

1. Films—The student observes under the guidance of his instructor a film of actual classroom situations, not necessarily the ideal one of loving teacher and adoring children. A discipline problem arises. How will the teacher handle it? A child asks an embarrassing question or deliberately tries to put his teacher on the spot. What happens? How will the teacher react?

The young people watching the film have an opportunity to see real situations they'll soon meet in their own classrooms. Then they discuss with the instructor the ways in which they might have met these specific problems.

2. One-way window watching—This type of window is being installed in some of the new buildings. A college instructor or a school supervisor brings in a group of student teachers to watch a live demonstration during which the children are unaware that

they are on exhibit. There's a great advantage here as the children act more naturally and the observers can ask questions without disturbing the routine of the class. (Let's hope the poor teacher has been told in advance!)

SOME IDEAS THAT ARE BEING TRIED

1. An internship of a year when the young "trainee" works with a master teacher, learns about planning, sees actual discipline problems, meets the parents, is present at faculty meetings, shares the duties—in short, shares the work of the school day.

2. An experienced teacher has the responsibility of guiding several new appointees. There are meetings with them, opportunities to observe veterans at work, facing real classroom problems under the guidance of one who has been through the mill. Naturally the guiding teacher would receive extra compensation and more free periods for the necessary planning and consultations.

3. Alternating six months of teaching with six months of graduate work with pay. There are many variations of this plan. In some instances the new teacher makes an agreement with the local school authorities which guarantees that if alternate teaching and study are arranged, with pay, the one in training agrees to teach in their schools for a specified length of time.

We are coming to the realization that the reason for the high dropout rate with new teachers is that they find the first year so hard, discouraging, and unexpectedly rough that the girls decide to try marriage and the boys look for other lines of work. More thorough preparation, more status in the professional world, and more money would change the picture.

—— THESE IDEAS WORKED FOR ME ——

Join your local teachers' organization. Be an active member. This does not mean that you must be a leader; good followers are important too, and they learn just as much.

Join a statewide or national teachers' organization. An active group such as this keeps you in touch with the efforts being made in behalf of better teaching and better teaching conditions. It's a clearing house for the profession.

Subscribe to a magazine for teachers. The articles are valuable and the planned lessons, pictures, and seasonable suggestions are very helpful. They keep you from getting in a rut.

Take in-service courses if they are provided by your Board of Education. Sometimes you *have* to take them to receive your salary increase. In any case take a course you *need* rather than one that's convenient or just plain easy.

If it is at all possible take a summer course at a university. Few of us can spend all our summers this way, but try to do it at least once every few years. Perhaps you can arrange to take an evening course at a university near home.

Keep a scrapbook. How often we wish we had kept a clipping from a newspaper, an up-to-the-minute picture, accounts of current doings in fields that are interesting to us. Reading, then cutting and pasting in a scrapbook, is important to our work, and sometimes points out to us our growing interest in a new field.

"Pad and Points"—Before you interview a parent or have a talk with your principal, even before making a telephone call, jot down on a handy pad the points you want to cover. It's surprising how much respect your opinions get when a person realizes you have fortified and prepared yourself in this way. Your added confidence shows.

Index